WARTIME
ON THE
RAILWAYS

WARTIME
ON THE
RAILWAYS

DAVID WRAGG

SUTTON PUBLISHING

First published in 2006 by
Sutton Publishing Limited · Phoenix Mill
Thrupp · Stroud · Gloucestershire · GL5 2BU

British Library Cataloguing in Publication Data
A catalogue record for this book is available from the British Library.

ISBN 0-7509-4246-0

Typeset in 10/13 pt New Baskerville.
Typesetting and origination by
Sutton Publishing Limited.
Printed and bound in England by
J.H. Haynes & Co. Ltd, Sparkford.

CONTENTS

List of Illustrations

Air-raid drill, London Midland & Scottish temporary headquarters, Watford.
Signalwoman Daisy Cook.
Air-raid damage at Liverpool Street station, London.
Evacuees, Euston station.
Bomb damage, Paddington station, London.
Aftermath of an air-raid, Bank station, London, 1941.
Blackout on the Underground.
Air-raid shelter at Elephant & Castle Underground station.
Southern Railway steamer SS *Isle of Jersey* as a hospital ship.
Gun production at Southern Railway's Eastleigh Works.
Wearing gas masks at work.
Spitfire MkV, *Flying Scotsman*.
Evacuees, Surbiton, 1944.

Abbreviations

IWM   Imperial War Museum
NRM   National Railway Museum

INTRODUCTION

There comes a time when locomotives are more important
than guns.

General Erich von Ludendorff, 1918

From the American Civil War onwards, railways have always played an
important part in warfare. While the first interest taken by the military in
railways in Britain during the mid-nineteenth century was primarily for
internal security purposes, by the end of that century the Boer War in
southern Africa saw a massive movement of men and their horses via the
London & South Western Railway and its port at Southampton. So
important were the railways that in the First World War the state took
control of them, and then repeated this exercise under somewhat more
controversial arrangements on the outbreak of the Second World War.

Wartime on the Railways is an account of the part played by Britain's
railways during the Second World War, dealing not simply with
operational matters or the impact of enemy action on the railways, but
also looking at financial arrangements, the part played by railway
workshops in producing equipment for the military and the wartime
experience of the railways' ships, with the narrative augmented by
personal accounts from railwaymen. It also shows how the war years saw
many jobs traditionally handled by men taken over by women. Not
forgotten is the role played by the London Underground, not least in
providing air-raid shelters at its deep-level Tube stations, although even
these were not as safe from the Luftwaffe's bombs as the many Londoners
using them believed.

ONE NIGHT IN MAY

On the morning of 11 May 1941, Mr Greenfield, station master at Waterloo, London's largest railway terminus, walked along the line from his station to Clapham Junction. It was a bright and sunny spring morning, but not in London. The heavy pall of smoke that hung in the air masked the sunshine, and everywhere there fluttered fragments of burned paper from the many fires. Overwhelming everything was the choking stench of burning. Earlier, trains carrying the national morning newspapers, that were such a feature of night working at Waterloo, had had to start from the suburban main-line stations of Wimbledon and Surbiton. The daily rush of commuters had to alight at Clapham Junction and use a special replacement bus service, but this could not cope as the road leading to Waterloo was cluttered with fire hoses; at one stage, the queue for the railway replacement buses stretched for more than a mile.

The previous night, the Luftwaffe had managed to close not only Waterloo, but also the other Southern Railway termini at Victoria, London Bridge, Charing Cross and Cannon Street, as well as King's Cross and St Pancras, the Waterloo & City Line, the Bakerloo Line, and the West End branch of the Northern Line.

In earlier centuries, warfare usually paused during the winter months as the belligerents turned their attention to surviving the worst of the weather. Growing mechanisation and new armaments meant that this changed during the twentieth century. Certainly, the winter of 1940–1 saw some of the worst weather in living memory, but it also saw the Germans continue to attack British towns and cities with unprecedented ferocity, for this was a modern war, and the prime component was air power. The German Luftwaffe had maintained its blitz of British cities from September, only missing a night if the weather intervened.

AIR RAIDS

Once spring arrived, with better weather, the prospect was of more and worse air raids, the only hope being that the shorter nights might make it more difficult for the Luftwaffe to mount heavy bombing raids over the entire country. Naturally enough, as the nation's capital and a vital point in the transport network, London had suffered most, but the Luftwaffe had also managed to pay a visit to most other major British cities. It had even reached those that pre-war had been regarded as relatively safe, such as Belfast. On the outbreak of war, children had been evacuated from the cities seen as being most at risk – even those in the west such as Glasgow, neighbouring Clydebank, and Liverpool – which showed considerable foresight on the part of the authorities, as the Luftwaffe attacked all of these places as well.

Aerial warfare had not come as a surprise. During the years between the two world wars, the belief had grown that 'the bomber would always get through'. Extensive air-raid precautions, or 'ARP' as they were commonly known, had been put in place well before the outbreak of hostilities, urged on by the fear that war might break out suddenly, with a surprise attack without a formal declaration of war. Under public pressure, the deep-level Tube stations of the London Underground had been opened up as additional air-raid shelters where people felt safe, but 'incidents', as serious damage by bombing was referred to in the official language of wartime, during October 1940 and January 1941 showed the public to have been over-optimistic. As early as October 1940, a bomb penetrated the Northern Line Tube station at Balham in south London, bringing down part of the tunnel and killing seventy-two people, of whom sixty-eight had been seeking shelter. In January 1941, another bomb pierced the road surface outside the Bank of England and the Royal Exchange in the heart of the City of London and exploded at the top of the escalators at Bank station, blowing out the windows of two Central Line Tube trains and wrecking the three escalators. Despite it being a Saturday evening and therefore quieter than on a busy week day, the explosion killed fifty-seven people and injured another sixty-nine. Other Tube stations also suffered. It seemed that nowhere was safe, and that the railways were the main target after the Luftwaffe had tried, and failed, to eliminate the Royal Air Force during the Battle of Britain.

Modern warfare soon showed that it was no respecter of status or rank. Lord Stamp, President of the London Midland & Scottish, the largest business in the British Empire, who had been leading the Railway Companies Association in their negotiations with the government, which wanted to revise its arrangements for the control and use of the railways in wartime, was killed with his family in an air raid during April. Indeed, the night of 16/17 April 1941 was one of the worst of the bombing campaign. In addition to the deaths of Lord and Lady Stamp and their eldest son, there were numerous other 'incidents', many of them on the railways.

This was the night that a landmine fell on the Hungerford Bridge, which carried the lines from Kent from what is now known as Waterloo East across the River Thames and into the Southern Railway terminus at Charing Cross, which itself was also badly damaged by bombs. Further east along the north bank of the River Thames, the lines into two other Southern termini, Blackfriars and Holborn Viaduct, were cut when a bomb demolished the bridge over Southwark Street on the south bank. A party of men working on the bridge sought refuge in a small metal shelter, but this was caught by the blast and three of them were killed.

The direct link between Waterloo station and the City of London was the Waterloo & City Line, the only deep-level Tube line owned and operated by a railway company by this time, but this too was put out of action when a bomb damaged an electricity sub-station at the Waterloo end. Popularly known by both its regular passengers and railwaymen as 'The Drain', the Waterloo & City was having a bad war, despite finally being favoured with new rolling stock specially built for it. It had already been closed after being flooded.

Further north on the other side of the City, the London Passenger Transport Board's Circle Line between Euston Square and King's Cross, shared with the Metropolitan Line at this point, was so badly damaged by bombing that it was put out of action for five months. Further west, near Marylebone station, the London goods depot of the former Great Central Railway was razed to the ground by incendiaries.

Given the growing use of parachute mines by the Luftwaffe, as well as their usual fare of high-explosive bombs and incendiaries, it was understandable that the Royal Navy feared that acoustic mines may have been laid on the bottom of the River Thames. On 19 April, all Underground lines running beneath the Thames had to be closed for a short period and shut off from the rest of the Tube network while the river was swept for mines. It was an oversight on the part of the Germans that they didn't find any.

THE WORST NIGHT

Waterloo station was Britain's largest railway terminus and also headquarters of the Southern Railway, a company whose business was overwhelmingly passenger traffic. Between 1910 and 1920 the station had been extensively rebuilt, becoming the world's first major terminus designed around the needs and the potential of the electric train.

In 1941, Waterloo handled trains for the south coast of England from Hampshire through to Devon, and then for the north coasts of both Devon and Cornwall, as well as suburban services to the western end of Surrey, Middlesex and Berkshire. Waterloo was the station for the soldier wishing to reach Aldershot, the home of the British Army, or its training grounds on Salisbury Plain. It was also the station for the sailor heading for Portsmouth or Gosport, although the matelot would have had the choice of the Southern or the Great Western if he was travelling to Portland or Plymouth. Waterloo was much less concerned with the airman, unless, of course, he was a naval one.

Approached from the road, Waterloo soared high above the surrounding buildings. It was reached by lines running mainly on viaduct and itself sat on top of large storage arches. It was a passenger station, with its goods traffic handled a short distance away at Nine Elms. Even in peacetime, not all of Waterloo's 'passengers' were alive; Waterloo included a Necropolis station for trains carrying the dead to Brookwood, a nineteenth-century development brought about as the growing metropolis outgrew its traditional burial grounds. In London, even the dead had to commute.

On the night of 10/11 May 1941, Waterloo was hit by at least fifty-one high-explosive and incendiary bombs and parachute mines. These set fires blazing and destroyed the Necropolis station. Worse, they penetrated the station floor and went down into the basement arches which were being used as a store for spirits. The resulting conflagration was such that the station was soon closed. The spirit store was not the only loss, as post office vans, motor horse boxes and even the chairman's car were all lost. The fire began soon after midnight and burned uncontrolled for two hours, as there was no water because the mains in Waterloo Road and York Road had burst. Some water was obtained from the locomotive supply at the station, but by 9 a.m. this was dry. When a fire brigade fire-fighting barge in the River Thames tried to direct its water jets towards the station, the supply proved intermittent. Another supply was discovered in the Waterloo & City Line sidings, and a pump was found, but it proved difficult to get the pump to the water. Eventually a crane was found and the pump was lowered from the surface workshops for the Waterloo & City. The water was pumped up 30ft, and then other pumps had to relay the water to the fire. Even then, while the fires in and around the station were gradually subdued, those in the arches continued and were not finally dampened down until 15 May. In the meantime, the station remained closed. It could only be partially reopened on 15 May, and it was mid-July before the terminus was fully operational again.

Far beneath the station, burst water mains meant that the Waterloo & City Line did not simply close with the terminus above. It was flooded so badly that it remained closed until 22 May.

On the other side of the river, Charing Cross had also had an eventful night. It all started when a high-explosive bomb landed on the Charing Cross Hotel at 1.50 a.m. and around a hundred incendiaries landed on the station itself, setting off fires everywhere with three trains blazing in the station and another on fire on Hungerford Bridge. Anticipating trouble, the station's fire-fighting team already had their pump armed up and ready, but they then had to climb on the roofs of the carriages of the trains in the station to fight the fires. They managed to douse all the flames by 3.10 a.m.

In the meantime, between 2 a.m. and 3 a.m., a porter had discovered a landmine hanging with its parachute entangled in the ironwork of the Hungerford Bridge, close to the signal-box with the signalman still working inside it. At around the same time, a fresh fire was noticed under platform 4. The telephones were out of action and a messenger had to be sent to fetch the fire brigade. While they were waiting for the fire brigade, the fire under platform 4 started to edge towards the landmine. The order was given to evacuate the station, but the railwaymen fighting the fire decided to press on. Meanwhile, the signalman, a man of sixty-seven years with fifty-two years' service on the railway, stuck to his post, returning to the box after extinguishing two incendiaries on the bridge. Eventually, the fire brigade arrived and by the time they had extinguished the blaze it was just 12ft from the landmine.

The landmine itself was dealt with by a naval officer who arrived with three ratings. The officer needed to communicate with the Admiralty at one point, and had to walk there and back! The landmine was defused by 10.30 a.m., and then was lifted by crane and taken away. At this stage they discovered that it weighed more than 3,100lb.

While this was going on, Cannon Street, the Southern Railway's main terminus for the City, was also being bombed. The station had restricted opening hours during the war, and at night was used to store rolling stock. Here, the bombs had started to fall at about 11 p.m., again with a combination of high explosive and incendiaries. The station foreman and a lineman had to step onto the bridge over the River Thames to put out incendiaries. On their return, they discovered that two bombs had fallen by a platform and incendiaries had set the station roof alight, while the station hotel was also on fire. The bombs destroyed the station's all-over roof, and so damaged the supporting walls that later the roof could not be reinstated. Railwaymen had to brave pieces of the roof falling onto them to rescue locomotives and carriages, but as one of the locomotives, *St Lawrence*, steamed out to the comparative safety of the bridge over the Thames, it too was caught by a bomb and destroyed. Another bomb missed the bridge and exploded in the river, sending water spurting over the signal-box.

Also in the City, another Southern terminus, Holborn Viaduct, was hit by bombs. They hit both the station itself and the adjoining hotel building, which by this time was being used as offices. The resultant fire completely gutted the station and, despite the normal frantic wartime pace of repair and reconstruction, including a temporary booking office, it could not be used again by trains until 1 June.

THE SOUTHERN WAS NOT ALONE

The Southern Railway was not the only victim that night. Two of the other main-line companies, the London Midland & Scottish (LMS) and the London & North Eastern Railway (LNER), also suffered.

The main LNER terminus at King's Cross was struck early in the morning of 11 May by two 1,000lb bombs chained together. These hit the west side of the station, demolishing part of the general offices, a grill room and a bar, completely destroying the booking hall. Twelve men were killed. Despite this destruction, it was a Sunday and fewer trains than usual were running, so it was not necessary to close the station. In addition to clearing up the rubble and making repairs, temporary booking and refreshment facilities were soon ready.

The situation at St Pancras across the road separating it from King's Cross was far worse. The LMS terminus had already lost a large part of its roof in an earlier landmine explosion, but during the night of 10/11 May, a bomb penetrated the floor of the station at the inner end of platform 3, passed through the vaults used for storing beer, and exploded close to the railway tunnel below. The main-line station itself was closed for eight days, but platforms 2 and 3 could not be used again until early June.

The damage that night was not confined to the major London termini. Elsewhere on the Southern Railway, the station at Elephant & Castle was badly damaged, with the island platform and up local platforms burned out. Repairs here were given a lower priority than at the major termini, so it was not until a temporary up main platform was built that the station could reopen on 1 September.

At Waterloo, the damage also had an impact on the London Underground, closing the Bakerloo Line and the West End branch of the Northern Line.

Those involved were not to know that relief was at hand. The period of nightly heavy bombing was coming to an end, as the bulk of the Luftwaffe was diverted eastwards for the invasion of the Soviet Union.

CHAPTER 2

RAILWAYS AND WARFARE

Someone once declared that the railways were the sole invention that had been of unquestioned benefit to mankind. The contrast was being made with the aeroplane, as much an instrument of war as a mode of transport in peacetime. It was certainly true that the railways did not seek a role for themselves in warfare, while the Admiralty and the War Office were initially deliberately hostile to the approach of the railways at Portsmouth and Shoeburyness respectively. On the other hand, a straw in the wind was that as early as 1842 legislation was passed that allowed the government emergency powers over the railways.

At the time, the primary reason for this growing government interest in the railways was internal security. It was not until invasion fears arose again in 1859 that consideration was given to the use of the railways in wartime. There was even the proposal that London should have a circular line built around it so that armoured trains carrying artillery could defend the capital. Sadly, this proposal for an 'iron road M25' came to nothing, as it could have been very useful in peacetime as well as during war. The nation's capital might have North, South, Western Extension and East London lines, but these do not interconnect, and, except for the East and North London lines, would have difficulty in doing so.

None of this should be too surprising as the American Civil War raged between 1861 and 1865, and showed that the railways were of supreme importance to army commanders. One reason why this was America's bloodiest war – apart from the obvious one that it was Americans fighting Americans – was that army commanders could have the men and the materiel that they wanted, wherever they wanted it and when they wanted it. What was more, troops arrived ready to fight, rather than tired from a lengthy forced march. It was easier to keep armies supplied, and the size of armies grew as it became possible to cope with their massive appetites for food and ammunition. On the plus side, the wounded could also be moved away more speedily and with less risk of further injury from being bounced around in a wagon over indifferent roads.

Before long, parliamentary scrutiny of legislation authorising new lines began to take defence requirements into account. Having originally rejected the London Tilbury & Southend Railway's extension to Shoeburyness in 1877, the War Office accepted the extension in 1882. The military was anxious that its ability to move men and war materiel rapidly would not be hampered by unnecessary problems on the railways, such as a break of gauge. This meant that the War Office joined those opposed to the Great Western Railway's broad gauge, which had upset many, mainly freight shippers, over the years. However, by this time not only were the days of the broad gauge already numbered, but the GWR also had a growing standard gauge network as well.

This concept of a standard gauge did not stop a British army engineer giving the railways in Ireland a different gauge, however. The story goes that he had to choose between a gauge of 5ft, as on the Great Eastern initially, and one of 5ft 6in, and decided to compromise at 5ft 3in. The mainland standard gauge seems to have been completely overlooked. The best one can say about this decision was that it was taken before the days of train ferries!

Even so, the emergency powers available at this time simply gave the government of the day the authority to direct how the railways should be run, leaving operational control in the hands of the companies. This remained the case with the legislation of 1844 and 1867, and even with the Regulation of the Forces Act 1871. Further recognition of the importance of the railways to the military included the creation of the Engineer & Railway Staff Volunteer Corps in 1865, so that experienced railwaymen would be on hand when needed. In 1896, an Army Railway Council was established, which later became the War Railway Council.

When war eventually did come, it was far off and no real threat was posed to the security of the United Kingdom. The railways had played a minor role in the Crimean War, although its supply needs swallowed up shipping. It was the Boer War that saw the British Army make extensive use of the railways, but this was confined to the workings of one company, the London & South Western Railway (LSWR), with the majority of troops sent to Southampton to embark for South Africa between 1899 and 1902 travelling through London's Waterloo station, while the cavalry took their horses with them through Nine Elms. This was no light task. Over three years, no fewer than 528,000 men were moved over the LSWR to Southampton, and in one of the first highly mobile wars, fought before the internal combustion engine achieved reliability, a substantial number of horses were carried as well.

Nevertheless, in contrast with the two global conflicts of the twentieth century, throughout the Boer War the LSWR remained under the control of its own management.

The big lesson of the Boer War was that concentrating so much traffic on London was inefficient, and in the years leading up to the outbreak of the First World War in 1914, the railway links between the coast and the military training and rear concentration areas on Salisbury Plain were improved.

While wartime demands could place a major strain on the railways, it was also the case that railway companies with major defence installations along their lines benefited from the traffic so generated. A good example was the so-called 'Portsmouth Direct', the line running between Waterloo and Portsmouth via Guildford. As weekenders returned to Waterloo on a Sunday evening, their trains were eagerly awaited by naval personnel returning to their ships after a weekend in town. It was rare, and remains so, for any railway to have its trains fully occupied in both directions at the same time of day.

THE FIRST WORLD WAR

War in Europe was unwelcome, while the manner of its coming was not anticipated but was widely expected. In political as well as business life it was an interruption to the normal state of affairs. The Liberal government had begun to consider nationalisation of the railways, but this was put aside as war loomed. Nevertheless, the state took far more extensive powers over the railways than had ever been anticipated, with the President of the Board of Trade, whose department was responsible for the railways, as well as ports and shipping, taking control of the railways and acting as nominal chairman of the Railway Executive Committee (REC), formed as early as 1912, to run the railways on behalf of the government. Membership of the REC included the general managers of the ten most important railway companies, and one of their number, Herbert Ashcombe Walker, general manager of the London & South Western Railway since 1910, was chosen as acting chairman, despite being one of the youngest general managers. It could have been the LSWR's experience of the demands of the military during the Boer War that had resulted in Walker becoming acting chairman, or it could have been the common-sense argument that since so much traffic would travel over the company's metals and it owned the port of Southampton, that it would be best placed to coordinate matters and liaise with both the Army and the Royal Navy. Either way, everything suggests that Walker was a great success in this post, for which he received a knighthood in 1917.

The REC's remit initially only covered railways in Great Britain, and it was not until 1917 that the Irish railway companies also came under its control – Ireland at that time being united and all of it part of the United Kingdom. Only one of the Irish railways, the Northern Counties Committee, was owned by a 'mainland' railway, the Midland Railway. The Great Southern & Western had a close relationship with the Great Western Railway, but it was a working relationship, not a financial arrangement. Control of the railways in Ireland was necessary not just for the war effort, but also because of the deteriorating internal security situation.

Of course, the LSWR had no monopoly of cross-Channel traffic, which was also shared with three other railway companies, the Great Eastern (GER), the South Eastern & Chatham (SECR), with its ports at Dover and Folkestone, and the London, Brighton & South Coast Railway (LBSCR), with its port at Newhaven. The LSWR operated cross-Channel and Channel Islands services from Southampton, while the Great Western also operated to the Channel Islands from Weymouth. While these cross-Channel routes put the companies in the front line, it was also important to remember that other shipping services were bringing men and horses across the Irish Sea, with Ireland an important source for both at the time, while the entire railway network was pressed into service to meet the needs of industry as well as the armed forces. There was some innovation during the First World War, with train ferries introduced between a new port at Richborough in Kent and France to help speed deliveries of rolling stock. This was not the first train ferry, as the concept had been pioneered many years earlier with a short-lived service between Hayling Island and Bembridge on the Isle of Wight, but it was the first practical application.

Few had any real idea of how modern warfare would affect the railways. The shelling of east coast towns by German naval forces was not unexpected, although no one had really considered by just how much naval gunnery had increased in potency over the previous century. Only a few considered attack from the air to be a serious threat, but as early as October 1914 the SECR had a lookout posted on Hungerford Bridge, carrying the line from London Bridge and what is now Waterloo East (then known as Waterloo Junction) into Charing Cross. The lookout was not expecting bombers but raiding Zeppelin airships, and if one was spotted no trains were to be allowed onto the bridge.

In fact, there was little damage to the railways from bombing during the First World War, despite their being recognised by both sides as legitimate and significant targets. Aircraft were in their infancy, and even a Zeppelin could only carry a limited load. Most of the action affected Liverpool Street. On the night of 8/9 September 1915, several bombs fell on the station, damaging the suburban and through lines, and fracturing a water main that flooded the suburban tracks. Nevertheless, partly because of the small size of the bombs, repairs were put in hand and a full service was restored by 11 a.m. on 9 September. The bombs also demolished a wall and shattered glass at Broad Street next door, where some horses were injured.

From the railway point of view, the most significant incident was in London during the air raid of 13 June 1917. The City of London was the target that day, and again three bombs landed on the Great Eastern's terminus at Liverpool Street: one of the bombs was a dud and failed to explode, another exploded on a platform and a third hit the dining car of the noon express to King's Lynn and Hunstanton, setting it alight. Two carriages between platforms 8 and 9 were being used for medical examinations, and these were smashed. All in all, sixteen people were killed and another thirty-six wounded, making it one of the worst bombing casualty rates in England during the First World War.

With commendable forethought, during the First World War the Great Northern Railway at King's Cross used Gas Works Tunnel as a shelter for main-line trains whenever enemy aircraft approached. This was perhaps the only benefit that the tunnel bestowed on the station, and, as would happen, the station was untroubled by German bombing during the war. This was just as well, as a massive volume of freight traffic passed through the station on its way to the SECR, including trainloads of explosives for the British forces fighting in France. A bomb hitting an ammunition train in the centre of a crowded metropolis was not something to have been taken lightly.

While we are concerned with Britain's railways, it is worth noting that the situation here was in complete contrast to the air raids on German marshalling yards in northern France and Belgium. Being situated closer to the enemy railway system, the Royal Naval Air Service and the Royal Flying Corps were able to inflict considerable damage on German communications in the final year of the war.

QUINTINSHILL

Unfortunately, accidents were a far more serious threat to the railways and those using them than enemy action. On 22 May 1915, Britain suffered its worst-ever railway disaster, with five trains involved, at least 227 people killed and another 245 injured. Most of those who died were soldiers on their way to France from Scotland, and as their unit records were destroyed in the fire that engulfed the wreckage, completely accurate figures have never become available.

The accident occurred at Quintinshill, near Carlisle, on the Caledonian Railway, although this was just another company within the ambit of the REC at the time. At Quintinshill, the signal-box covered not just the main line but also two passing loops to allow expresses to overtake the slower goods trains and local stopping trains. At the time both loops were occupied by goods trains, so that a northbound local train had to be reversed onto the southbound main line to allow what was in effect two expresses, running as one long train double-headed, to pass it on their way to Edinburgh and Glasgow. Unfortunately the local trrain was promptly forgotten about by the signalman. Towards this unhappy scene, a crowded troop train raced downhill from Beattock, with twenty-one carriages, mainly elderly six-wheelers largely of wooden construction and with gas lighting. It struck the local train with such force that it was compressed to a quarter of its original length. Worse was to follow, as the double-headed northbound expresses ran into the wreckage before they could stop. Glowing coals from the locomotive fireboxes created an inferno as they ignited the ruptured gas pipes for the lighting of the troop train. The resultant fire was so severe that it did not die down for twenty-four hours.

The background to the accident was that the night signalman had been due to hand over to his relief at 6 a.m., but the relief travelled on the local passenger train from Gretna and did not arrive until 6.30 a.m. The relief signalman had in fact arrived in the box at the time of the accident, but instead of taking over his duties he was busily engaged in writing up the register of train movements from 6 a.m. onwards in his own hand to hide the fact that he had been late for duty. The signal-box was also by this time fairly crowded with some of the crews of the two goods trains, while the fireman from the local train was there to sign the register to state that his train was standing on the upline. Unfortunately, the fireman omitted to ensure that the signalman had put reminder collars on the lever of the signal protecting the train. The signalman also failed to send a signal, using a bell code, to the next signal-box to the north at Kirkpatrick, which could have stopped the troop train. Worse, he accepted the troop train and then offered it to Gretna. The stage was set for a major accident.

The accident did little to endear the railways to the public. The troop train was composed of obsolete rolling stock set aside for the purpose with little protection for the occupants in even a minor accident. While both signalmen were negligent and convicted of manslaughter, the real culprit was the railway company, which had failed to pay for any form of automatic train control.

STATE CONTROL

The objective of state control of the railways was to ensure that the system operated as one. In one sense, this was an excessive measure as the pre-war railways had coordinated themselves very well indeed, partly through the workings of the Railway Clearing House, which did more than simply balance inter-company tickets and freight receipts. Several companies could, and did, collaborate, especially to ensure the smooth through running of the Anglo-Scottish expresses, of which the most complicated was that from Aberdeen to Penzance, a distance of well over 800 miles.

What did emerge, however, was a system that enabled resources to be directed to wherever they might be most needed, rather than companies keeping their equipment to themselves while another part of the system suffered under wartime pressures. One of these pressures was, of course, the fact that many railwaymen had volunteered to join the armed forces, while others were mobilised because of their reserve obligations. In fact, during the First World War, no fewer than 184,475, 45 per cent of railwaymen of military age, had enlisted. The military had also helped itself to locomotives and rolling stock for service as far away as Mesopotamia.

Despite cutting or reducing many ordinary services to free men and equipment for military use, there were increased pressures on the system over and above the obvious need for troop trains. Unforeseen by the planners on the outbreak of war was that the role of coastal shipping, in peacetime so important for the movement of bulk commodities such as coal, was severely restricted by enemy activity in the North Sea and the English Channel.

Few warships were fuelled by oil at this stage in the Royal Navy's history, because of fears that sufficient oil might not be available in wartime. The Grand Fleet had moved to its forward wartime base at Scapa Flow in Orkney, not the most convenient location for supply by railway, and so coal had to be carried from South Wales to Grangemouth, where it was transferred to coastal shipping, on the so-called 'Jellicoe Specials', named after the commanding admiral. No fewer than 13,630 coal trains were run for this purpose alone between August 1914 and March 1919, with Pontypool Road on the Great Western Railway being the main loading point. Grangemouth had to be the main trans-shipment point because further north the railways, with most of the route mileage single track, could not have coped, and there were insufficient port facilities in the far north of Scotland. Despite the shortcomings of the largely single-tracked line north of Perth, naval manpower was moved further north by rail, putting the Highland Railway under great strain between Perth and Inverness and then north to Thurso. This required 'naval specials' to be operated every night, covering the 717 miles from Euston to Thurso in 21½ hours, an average speed of just over 33 miles per hour!

Such was the volume of traffic across the Channel that a new port had to be built at Richborough, close to Sandwich in Kent, despite the closure to civilian traffic of both Dover and Folkestone. Train ferries were introduced to carry war materiel across the Channel, and also to help move locomotives and rolling stock. More than 600 locomotives were pressed into military service overseas, as the half inch or so difference between British and French track gauges mattered little. Routine operations were severely affected as railway workshops were converted to help with the war effort, including the manufacture of armaments, while rolling stock was converted to provide ambulance trains. Some minor railway lines, as far apart as near Dumfries in the south-west of Scotland and at Southsea on the south coast, were closed in wartime never to reopen, but the creation of new manufacturing plant, such as an ordnance factory near Gretna close to the border between Scotland and England, also meant that additional facilities had to be created quickly.

The number of line closures was in fact relatively limited and the impact on the community very slight, but economy in manpower, fuel and materials all meant that services elsewhere had to be reduced. There were fewer trains, and as the Gretna accident showed, many were lengthened or combined, while overall speeds were reduced, although none of these measures was as restrictive as those imposed during the Second World War. Dining car and sleeping car provision was also reduced, but again, the cuts were not as severe as those that came in the early 1940s and these facilities never quite disappeared completely. First-class travel survived the war years, even on inner suburban lines and those parts of the London Underground offering this facility, but eventually cheap day return tickets were withdrawn to discourage leisure travel.

New, rebuilt or reconditioned steam locomotives appeared in a drab grey colour scheme, or perhaps 'colourless scheme', although one would have thought that all-over black would have been just as utilitarian and perhaps more serviceable.

Despite it being a truly global war, the main centre of activity was in Europe, and the greatest pressure fell on the Channel ports, with first Dover and then Folkestone closed to civilian traffic. The South Eastern & Chatham Railway became Britain's front-line railway, with the heaviest responsibility for the movement of men and materials to the coast. In London, Charing Cross also had the role of being Westminster's local station, and a special train, code-named *Imperial A*, was held ready at all times for VIP journeys to the coast, being used for 283 journeys during the war years. This was a short-formed but luxurious operation, usually consisting of just a Pullman car and a brake composite. A military staff officers' train operated daily from Charing Cross to Folkestone, leaving at 12.20.

At the other end of the scale, Charing Cross was the arrival point for many of the casualties of war. Perhaps the best example of this was on 7 June 1917. After the start of the Battle of Messines at dawn, the first wounded arrived at Charing Cross at 2.15 p.m. the same day.

Nevertheless, the state was in the position of having power over the railways, but without any long-term responsibility for their technical or financial health. It was to prove to be a short-sighted and improvident proprietor. Had the state been an active operator with the interest of the railway network in mind, it could have diverted resources to easing many of the bottlenecks emerging on the system under wartime pressures.

Financially, the war years were a disaster for the railway companies. This was despite the levels of compensation being based on pre-war earnings, as the years immediately before the outbreak of war had been ones of prosperity for the United Kingdom, and the railways had shared in this. Post-war, one general manager noted that the combined profits for the railway companies in 1913 had totalled £45 million, but that by

1920 these had dropped to less than £7 million, owing to improved rates of pay during First World War when the railways were under direct government control. By 1921, immediately before government control ceased, the railways were running at a loss overall of around £9 million. Part of the reason was almost certainly the cost of manpower. Railway wages in 1913 had totalled £47 million, but by 1920 had risen to £160 million. This was a clear example of the state having power without responsibility. It is also possible that this poor financial position was one reason why calls for nationalisation were dropped.

LONGMOOR MILITARY RAILWAY

The importance of the railways during the First World War was such that the military built a network of narrow-gauge lines behind the Western Front to move supplies and troops. The lessons were learned by all the belligerents, but post-war only the victors were in a position to do anything about it, even though funds were short.

Almost as a postscript to the British Army's experience of railway operation and the importance of railways in wartime was the Longmoor Military Railway (LMR). This was one of the most significant military railways to survive between the two wars. Originally founded as the Woolmer Instructional Railway for training members of the Royal Engineers in railway operation and maintenance, the LMR also had the potential to serve the large base area around Bordon in Hampshire. It linked the Waterloo to Portsmouth main line, known in railway circles as the 'Portsmouth Direct', at Liss with a branch line at Bordon, and in between a substantial network developed. The line was sufficiently important to have been kept open by the British Army, which by this time had created a Royal Corps of Transport, until 1970.

In its heyday the LMR operated a stud of tender locomotives and a number of 0–6–0ST, or saddle tanks, with ex-civilian railway passenger carriages painted blue. All of the locomotives, no matter how humble, were named. Many of them were bargains, including 0–6–2T *Thisbe*, acquired by the Woolmer Instructional Railway in 1914 after its original owners, the Shropshire Light Railway, found it too heavy for their needs.

Other military railways included one on Salisbury Plain.

CHAPTER 3

PEACE AND POVERTY

Post-war, the railways were not handed back to their proprietors until 1921, by which time major changes were in hand.

The first of these was in governmental responsibility for the railways. It was clear that the railways had outgrown the Board of Trade, and in 1919 a new department of state, the Ministry of Transport, was created. Sir Eric Geddes became the first Minister of Transport and, for the first and last time, the nation's railways had someone at government level who knew something about their business. Geddes had joined the North Eastern Railway in 1904 at the age of twenty-nine, becoming deputy general manager of the company by 1914. Despite the new department being one of the least senior in the government, the new minister had grand ideas for reorganising and streamlining Britain's transport system, including the railways, and indeed his ideas even extended to the supply of electricity. So grand were his ideas that he did not even bother to consult the railway companies about their future.

Once again, nationalisation was one of the options considered, but instead it was decided to reduce the large number of small railway companies. A report recommended that there should be seven companies, but this was eventually changed to just four, ostensibly to ensure greater coordination and less competition, but still the Aberdeen–Penzance service would require inter-company cooperation. This grouping was authorised by the Railways Act 1921, by which time Geddes must have known that he would not remain to see the scheme through to fulfilment in 1923, as in 1922 he left to join the board of Dunlop, the tyre and rubber products manufacturer, becoming its chairman, and in 1924 he became part-time chairman of the new Imperial Airways. The cynics who define a 'whizz kid' as someone who moves on before his mistakes catch up with him would see in Geddes a prime example, for after all, he not only left the new MoT, but he actually changed sides, leaving the railways and moving to firms with interests in road transport and aviation!

For the railways, whether or not they were legislated for and supervised by the Board of Trade or the new Ministry of Transport was academic. What was far from academic was the need for the companies to reorganise

18

themselves into four large groups. They had to cope with wartime arrears of maintenance and a perilous financial situation while thinking about how to make the new structures work. The legislation had side-stepped this, by simply creating 'Southern', 'Western', 'North Western, Midland and Scottish' and 'North Eastern, Eastern and Eastern Scottish' groups. In some cases, the situation was eased by the fact that many of the minor lines were already worked by larger neighbours, despite being nominally independent. In the case of the Western Group, 80 per cent of the route mileage already belonged to just one company, the Great Western, which simply absorbed its neighbours, although, to its dismay, it found that some of them were classified not as subsidiary companies but as constituent companies, with the right to a seat on the new company's board.

The grouping was not as neat as it might sound. If reduced competition and greater coordination were sought, why did the old London, Tilbury & Southend Railway (LTSR) service belong to the London Midland & Scottish when there was a competitive service from Liverpool Street, formerly Great Eastern but by this time London & North Eastern Railway? The fact that the LTSR had been taken over by the Midland Railway, one of the two main constituent companies of the LMS, suggests that the parliamentarians were less than diligent in their tidying up. There was overlap, with South Wales being predominantly Great Western, but with a considerable penetration by the LMS. The Southern and the Great Western competed between London and Exeter, and the Great Western and the LMS between London and Birmingham, while the LNER and the LMS competed between London and Manchester. The two largest companies, the LMS and the LNER, competed between London and Scotland, and both expended much of their energy and technical effort in competing on the Anglo-Scottish routes, producing prestigious trains running at high speed.

The only beneficial aspect of this failure to achieve substantial rationalisation was that when war came, or more particularly once the bombing started, the maze of routes and connecting lines meant that it was rare for anywhere to be cut off completely. Rare, but not entirely unknown, as both Liverpool and Coventry were to find out.

While an entire year, 1922, was devoted to the arrangements necessary to make grouping work, there were no objections to companies who wanted to get together sooner. The London & North Western Railway had long wanted to acquire the Lancashire & Yorkshire Railway, but its advances had been rejected and would in any case have needed parliamentary approval, which could not be guaranteed, but the two companies became one in 1922 well before the official date. The Great Western took over the passenger operations of the Taff Vale Railway, again ahead of grouping. In case of any dispute, a tribunal existed to arbitrate. Even once grouped, the railways weren't free from state control. The grouping established that there would be set standard revenues for each company based on their immediate post-war annual turnover, while charges to passengers and freight customers were controlled by the Railway Rates Tribunal. Charges were not set on any simple basis but instead varied between commodities. A 'common carrier' obligation also existed, that stipulated that the railways must carry whatever traffic was offered. In fact, the railways were by far the most regulated mode of transport in the country until the first of the road traffic acts reached the Statute Book in 1930.

Despite the fact that the railways were never to achieve the standard revenue predicted by the legislation, there was to be constant political pressure on them to modernise and to keep their infrastructure and rolling stock in good repair, just in case of another war. The years of conflict had placed a heavy demand on the railways. The state had been a weak manager, but it was left to the railway companies to put matters right, and their shareholders had to bear the pain.

YEARS OF STRIFE

The end of the First World War had come after the Bolshevik Revolution in Russia, and while many countries in the Russian Empire – notably Finland and Poland – took advantage of the troubles and the civil war that followed it to seize their independence, the revolution came as a severe shock to those living in the democracies. Bolshevik-style uprisings in a number of countries in continental Europe, and what would later become known as national socialist, or 'fascist', counter-movements unsettled many elsewhere. Labour unrest was viewed as suspect.

Much of this fear and suspicion was wild and unnecessary, but it underlines the trauma experienced by those who had lived through the upheaval in Russia and also seen much of Ireland achieve home rule after what was, by British standards, a bloody uprising. As events were to show, some concern over unrest was justified, but for the most part it was exaggerated. Even so, when A.B. MacLeod went to the Isle of Wight in

1928 to take charge of the Southern Railway's Locomotive, Carriage and Wagon Department on the island, he was warned of trouble:

> My predecessor met me and after a hurried lunch seemed anxious to leave as soon as possible for the mainland. We did, however, go down to the headquarters of the Department which was at Ryde St John's Road, where I was warned that I must remember that I was an 'Overner' and not an Islander and would have difficulty with the staff, some of whom were alleged to have Bolshevik tendencies . . .

MacLeod's narrative then showed how, for many at the time, the situation could easily descend from the sublime to the ridiculous. He was asked if he could solve an urgent problem.

> 'You see, it's like this,' the locomotive foreman said. 'The leading engine fitter caught an owl in the erecting shop this morning and won't let it go because he wants to sell it to a taxidermist for stuffing.' 'Why don't you let it go?' I said. 'Well, you see the fitter is a Bolshevik and very difficult,' he replied.

> (*Rails in the Isle of Wight*, P.C. Allen and A.B. MacLeod, London, George Allen and Unwin, 1967)

Ignoring the paradox that a declared Bolshevik should be contemplating a foray into capitalism, the conversation seems almost surreal to us today, but tells us much about attitudes at the time. In fact, all MacLeod did was find the fitter and give him a stiff reminder about cruelty to birds and the fact that he was not paid to catch birds in the company's time. He was then sent away to clean off the oil on the bird with paraffin and release it into a nearby wood.

In fact, even before the miners' strike of 1926 and the related General Strike that followed, industrial disputes simmered away. There was an earlier miners' strike in 1921. Typical of the state of industrial relations at the time was a strike by shunters on the Great Western Railway at Swansea in early 1924. The miners' strike began early in May 1926, and on 3 May many railwaymen joined the General Strike called by the Trades Union Congress in support of the mineworkers. Transport was badly affected, and the railway companies called for volunteers, many of them from the general public, to help run the railways. The General Strike lasted just nine days as members of the public, company management with first-hand experience of many of the skilled jobs, and troops all came together to try to keep the country running. Afterwards, it was claimed that many of the novice railwaymen had become proficient in just two days, but it was also true that the dispute had cost the companies a substantial sum – the Great Western alone estimated its losses at £1.8 million. Even after the return to work, the industrial situation and the supply of coal remained uncertain, with further financial losses as the mines remained closed. Afterwards, the industrial unrest continued, and on the Great Western locomen and shunters at Swansea came out on strike again during August. The miners eventually returned to work in late November, but any hope that the British economy would return to normal was soon dashed.

The British coal mines had enjoyed a substantial export business, but this had been affected by the demands at home and the difficulties of providing shipping during wartime, then by worldwide recession, and finally the miners' strike. There was more coal available than customers needed, so much of the export business went to coal mines in Germany and elsewhere. Output from the South Wales mines alone slumped from 50 million tons annually to 35 million tons. This was to be another factor in stopping the railway companies achieving their standard revenues.

The miners had struck in protest at being expected to take pay cuts to ward off the impact of recession on their industry, but soon railwaymen were also being asked to take pay cuts. For much of the 1930s, reductions of between 1.25 and 2.5 per cent were expected of many railwaymen by their managements. Dividends disappeared for most of the 'Big Four' companies, with only the Great Western maintaining one, but that for 1938 slumped to just half of 1 per cent, the first time it had fallen below 3 per cent for seventy years. Some of the money for the Great Western dividends had come from reserves, but for shareholders in many of the other companies this was not an option. Only the Southern Railway and the Great Western showed any real indications of profitability during these years.

A look at the dividends paid before the First World War and in the years leading up to the Second World War is instructive. Taking the Southern Railway as an example, in 1912 the four companies that were to make up the Southern were mainly in profit, with the London & South Western paying a dividend of 5.62 per cent on its ordinary shares, while the London Brighton & South Coast paid 5 per cent, and of the two companies operated by the South Eastern & Chatham Managing Committee, the South Eastern paid 3.87 per cent, leaving the London Chatham & Dover to pay nothing. Yet by 1935, after extensive investment in successful electrification schemes, the Southern Railway could only pay 4 per cent on its preference stock while the ordinary, or deferred, shares received nothing. In 1936 the preference shares continued to attract 4 per cent and the ordinary stock received just 0.5 per cent. In 1937, the preference shares received 3 per cent and the ordinary 1.5 per cent, but this was a high point, because in 1938, although the preference shares received 4 per cent, once again the ordinary shares received nothing. Modernisation came at a high price if you were a holder of ordinary shares.

The Great Western Railway had also managed to pay 5.62 per cent in 1912, but the railway that gave the world what was for a short period the fastest scheduled daily service, 'The Cheltenham Flyer', could only pay 3 per cent by 1935. This was maintained in 1936, and then actually rose to 3.5 per cent the following year, before collapsing to 0.5 per cent in 1938. For the ordinary railway shareholder, a Post Office savings account must have seemed very attractive at times like this.

Of the companies that combined to form the London & North Eastern Railway, in 1912 the Great Eastern managed to pay 2.5 per cent and the Great Northern 4.37 per cent, with 6 per cent on the North Eastern, but the North British had struggled to pay 3 per cent on its preference stock and 1 per cent on its deferred stock, while the Great Central paid nothing. At least the latter's shareholders were prepared for what happened in the years 1935–8, when the LNER could not pay a dividend.

On the other side of the Pennines, of the companies that amalgamated to form the giant London Midland & Scottish, in 1912 the London & North Western paid a healthy 6.5 per cent, and even in Scotland there were dividends, with the Glasgow & South Western leading the way with 4.87 per cent, followed by the Caledonian at 3.75 per cent and the Highland at 2.25 per cent, while the Midland, famous for the comfort of its trains, was not too well rewarded for its care with just 2.5 per cent on its preference stock and 3.87 per cent on its deferred stock. The LMS was renowned for its adoption of modern American management practices, and it also sorted out some of the sillier practices of its predecessor companies, among which the Midland, for example, had tended to build only smaller locomotives, so that double-heading was frequently required, which, lacking the means of remote control usual on electric and diesel double- or multiple-headed locomotives, also doubled labour costs and did not make the best use of coal. Despite the modern management practices, the LMS failed to pay a dividend in 1935 and could only manage 1.25 per cent in 1936. Although this rose to 1.5 per cent in 1937, it disappeared again in 1938.

The Great War had been anything but 'great' for the railways and their shareholders, something that became all too apparent because for most of the companies mentioned, the dividends for 1913 were either the same as for 1912 or even better, with two exceptions, the London Chatham & Dover (LCDR) and the Great Central. How the LCDR shareholders must have wished that their company had been taken over by the South Eastern in 1891, and how they must have cursed their ancestors for their ambition in creating a rival to the SER all those years earlier, when it had seemed so important for Chatham to have its own railway while the South Eastern had seemed so keen on developing its railway south of the Weald. As for the Great Central, its management had been ambitious, too ambitious, and its shareholders must have resented the refusal of Parliament to allow its original planned merger with the Great Northern.

It would be unfair to describe railway stock in 1938 as junk bonds, but it took an act of faith, even of blind optimism, for anyone to consider investing in the railways.

THE PRESSURE TO MODERNISE

Between the wars, the main-line railway companies were under constant pressure to maintain their assets at a high standard, even though commercial logic would have suggested that the time for rationalisation was approaching. The railways had long since provided bus services for those travelling to and from their stations and the nearest towns and villages, and goods-haulage services had also been provided to collect and deliver customers' consignments, but in 1928, the railway companies had received the powers to operate road transport in their own right. In many cases, road transport was far better suited to the travelling needs of the public and the needs of the shipper. In fact, advertising by the LMS emphasised the point that in the late 1930s the company employed every mode of transport. This was no exaggeration, for apart from their own bus and road transport services, augmented by investment in independent companies and even competing long-distance and excursion coach operators, the railways had their ferry services and were also becoming heavily involved in air transport.

Despite the poor financial situation of the railways, the directors and managers of the four grouped companies had continued to maintain their railways to the best of their abilities, and had invested as heavily as they could, especially after the removal of taxation on passenger travel and the low-cost loans introduced in 1929. This was most obvious on the Southern Railway, although to some extent the introduction of more powerful steam locomotives necessary for the longer-distance services had taken second place to electrification. Even so, the Southern had tried its best to spread modernisation around its system. The Great Western as well had not simply been content to concentrate on its expresses, but had thought about the problems of rural branch lines with the introduction of its diesel railcars. Given the picture of poor returns, one can have some sympathy for the other two companies, running a limited number of expresses but not doing much for the rural and suburban lines. The LMS did at least have a substantial number of fine mixed-traffic locomotives, including the handsome and rightly famous Stanier 4–6–0s, or 'Black Fives', that were to be largely copied by the post-war nationalised railway, and which were equally at home on the lighter expresses, suburban trains or goods work.

Few today realise that railway travel was taxed by the government through the Railway Passenger Duty, which had first been introduced in 1832 and by the late 1920s was levied on all passenger fares above 1*d* per mile. In his Budget in 1929, the Chancellor of the Exchequer in Baldwin's Conservative administration, the then Mr Winston Churchill, announced the abolition of the Railway Passenger Duty, on condition that the sums realised were capitalised and used for railway modernisation. This was an attempt to reduce unemployment rather than improve the lot of the passenger.

Further measures intended to encourage more modernisation of the railways and effectively create work to stimulate the economy included the Guarantees and Loans Act 1934, which today would be regarded as an example of Keynesian economics and 'pump priming'. Regardless of how one feels about Keynes and his ideas, in practice here was yet another new incentive for the railways to modernise. In November 1935, the government agreed with the four main-line railway companies to provide funds for major improvement schemes at an interest rate of 2.5 per cent, lower than that generally available on the money markets at the time, through a Railway Finance Corporation, which would have its initial capital of £30 million (£1,800 million today) guaranteed by the Treasury. Once again we find the Southern, despite being by far the smallest of the railway companies, taking an ambitious approach, with a loan of £6 million (£360 million today) to fund further electrification and improvements at a number of stations, as well as construction of a new suburban branch line.

The main-line railways continued to intensify their modernisation programme, as the government had intended. In fact, much of the work was an extension of that already in hand. The Southern Railway, which had electrified its inner and then its outer suburban networks, had used the money released by the abolition of the passenger duty to embark on main-line electrification, starting with the line from London to Brighton. This was the company's shortest but busiest main line. By the outbreak of war in 1939, electrification had reached towns as far apart as Reading, Aldershot and Maidstone, while on the coast, the lines from London to Portsmouth and Eastbourne and everywhere in between, were electrified, and if travelling via Eastbourne, electric trains reached as far east as Hastings.

While the Southern Railway's preoccupation was with its passenger traffic, for uniquely within the 'Big Four' it was predominantly a passenger railway, the other three companies saw freight traffic as important. The fashion was for marshalling yards with 'humps' so that goods trains could be marshalled using gravity, although by 1939 most marshalling yards were still flat with a consequent high demand for shunting locomotives. The Great Western set about serious experiments with diesel railcars, and then with diesel shunting locomotives.

Both the LMS and the LNER engaged in some electrification, but the poverty-stricken LNER could not do what the Southern would have done and electrify its busy suburban lines from Liverpool Street and the Liverpool Street to Southend line. Plans were laid for electrification of the Liverpool Street suburban lines and the trans-Pennine route, but neither could be completed until after the war and nationalisation. Nor did the LMS keep its promise to the council at Southend and electrify its competing line from Fenchurch Street to Southend and Shoeburyness. It was cheaper to invest in powerful tank engines that, it was claimed, could accelerate as well as an electric train, and even perform better than an electric train if the rails were slippery! All three companies continued to develop and build new steam locomotives, but the LNER insisted on building in small batches and concentrated on its fast services to Scotland and the north of England. The LMS did experiment with diesel shunting locomotives and with what would now be described as a diesel multiple unit, while looking ahead to a diesel-electric locomotive for main-line use.

Modernisation was nevertheless patchy and even piecemeal. Not all of this was the fault of the railways. The Great Western Railway, for example, tried in vain to get its customers to use larger goods wagons, especially for coal and ore traffic, proposing first wagons of 20 tons capacity and then wagons of 40 tons, as against the 5 or 10 tons then commonplace. The larger wagons would also have been fully fitted, that is they would have had brakes operated by the locomotive, allowing a substantial increase in train speeds. Taken together, the higher-capacity wagons and higher speeds would have meant a substantial improvement in productivity, making the railways more competitive with road transport, and might even have transformed the economics of freight operation. It was not to be. The smaller wagons were better suited to the tight curves of the sidings close to the pitheads, and relaying these was out of the question. No doubt the economics of the coal-mining industry were at least as dire as those of the railways by this time, with markets lost in the wake of the miners' strike. Even so, the effect of the miners' strike and the general strike on the British economy between the wars was such that it became increasingly uncompetitive, while later the ability to provide the support that wartime industry needed was seriously compromised.

Nevertheless, the financial situation was far from rosy. A modest economic upturn in 1937 was accompanied by increased travel, due in no small part to the Coronation of King George VI and Queen Elizabeth that year, and this was one of the better years. Any optimism evaporated as 1938 proved to be a poor year. The increase in armaments production did not affect the demand for goods traffic sufficiently, while the Munich crisis kept people at home, fearing the worst.

The London Midland & Scottish provides a good example of just how the railway shareholders suffered during the years of the grouping. On 1 January 1925 the company's share price was 20s 3d for the ordinary stock, but this dropped to 6s in 1938, and then to 2s 8½d as it turned out that the year was to be a miserable one for the railways. The ordinary stockholders had received an unexciting dividend of 2 per cent in 1930, but received nothing at all for 1938.

The spectre of nationalisation would not go away, and a step towards this occurred in the London area during the early thirties, even though the main-line railways retained their own lines within London when, on 1 July 1933, the London Passenger Transport Board (LPTB) came into existence. In some ways this was an unusual decision, as the bus operators were not so fortunate, and many, including Thames Valley and Aldershot & District, had to transfer depots, vehicles and routes to the new organisation, while those operating entirely within the 2,000 square mile area of the LPTB were taken over completely, including a number of municipal operators. The new LPTB acquired the entire London Underground network, including the District Line that used some of the Southern Railway's metals, while the Bakerloo and the District used those of the LMS to reach Watford and Barking respectively. While a take-over of the suburban networks themselves might have posed operational difficulties, using the same tracks as longer-distance services from the main termini, it does seem strange in retrospect that the Hammersmith & City Line continued to be operated jointly between London Transport and the Great Western until it passed completely to London Transport in 1948, while the Southern Railway was able to hang on to the Waterloo & City Line, the 'Drain', until nationalisation, after which it remained with British Railways until 1994. It also seems strange that the lines of the North London Railway, at least those between Richmond and Broad Street, also remained in railway company hands. The most the LPTB did was take some of the LNER suburban lines for electrification and operation by Tube trains.

Intended from the outset as an integrated road and rail transport organisation for London, the London Passenger Transport Area stretched out as far as Windsor, Guildford, Horsham, Gravesend, Tilbury, Hertford, Luton and Dunstable. Within this area, all suburban railway services were to be coordinated by a Standing Joint Committee consisting of four LPTB members and the four main-line railway general managers, and all receipts from the area, less operating costs, were to be apportioned between the LPTB and the railways. The Southern Railway's share of these receipts was fixed at 25½ per cent, a tribute to the traffic growth generated by its investment in suburban electrification, by this time completed, but hardly an incentive to further modernisation. By contrast, at the other end of the scale, the Great Western's share of the receipts was just over 1 per cent, reflecting its limited suburban network.

This was only really the second major British nationalisation. The first was the acquisition of the telegraph systems, mainly operated by the railways, which became part of the Post Office. This had integrated a highly fragmented communications system and was an early and unqualified success. The actual running of the railways was different, as differing ownership had not prevented through running and many passengers as well as much freight travelled on the lines of a single company while many more miles were accounted for by groupings of companies such as the Cheshire Lines Joint Committee or the companies running the east and west coast Anglo-Scottish routes.

Between these two examples of state ownership lay a few minor examples, such as the creation of the British Broadcasting Corporation from the British Broadcasting Company, but this happened while broadcasting was still in its infancy. The compulsory amalgamation of four small airlines to form Imperial Airways in 1924 was in effect a state-subsidised company rather than nationalisation as such. Most, but by no means all, of the larger towns and cities had municipal public transport, which by this time could mean bus or trolleybus instead of trams, but this was always a local decision, not a matter for the government, which had simply granted local authorities the powers to compulsorily acquire these operators. In fact, private enterprise in urban public transport survived in a number of towns and cities, such as Oxford, Bristol, Hastings, Gosport and Fareham, while some local authorities had relinquished their tramway systems in favour of private enterprise, as in Poole.

Seeking a 'Square Deal'

The continued poor economic outlook for the railways and the still high level of competition from road transport, led to a campaign calling for a fair deal for the railways. The campaign was planned and promoted by the Railway Companies Association, the body representing the 'Big Four' railway companies, against what they saw as unfair competition from road transport. This was despite the fact that by this time they were allowed to engage in road transport, which had been followed by a succession of acts that had established licensing systems for first road haulage and then road passenger transport, allowing the railways to object to route licensing applications by bus operators.

The 'Square Deal' campaign proved to be a complete failure and was in any case soon overtaken by the preparations for war. The new Mass

Observation movement took the campaign as one of its first surveys of public attitudes in 1938, with what would be regarded by modern opinion polls as a massive survey of 6,450 people. This large sample were asked for their views on the effectiveness of the campaign and found that just a fifth of those surveyed were interested in the fate of the railways. Worse still, of this fifth, two-thirds were simply interested in such matters as wages or fares. No fewer than four-fifths had nothing relevant to say about the campaign.

CHAPTER 4

THE RAILWAYS IN 1939

While there are those who maintain that the railways in 1939 were of a generally high standard, the truth is that they were a very mixed collection of services. The very best express trains were often operating at speeds of 60mph, linking important centres and certainly offering better frequencies than at the time of the grouping, and indeed, better frequencies between major centres than could be found anywhere else in the world. There was also a pecking order among express trains. The 'Flying Scotsman' and the day 'Aberdonian' on the LNER, the 'Coronation Scot' on the LMS, and the 'Cheltenham Flyer' and 'Bristolian' on the GWR aspired to average speeds of 70mph, while the 'Cornish Riviera' offered superb wide-bodied vehicles and was so popular that in the summer months the train ran in several sections, or what we today might describe as 'reliefs', running long distances non-stop. It was true that anyone with urgent business could turn up at a station, buy a ticket and, except on commuter trains in the rush hours, find a comfortable seat on an express, enjoy a drink and a meal on the journey, and usually arrive punctually at their destination. On the LNER and LMS, even third-class passengers could expect to be seated six to a compartment, although on the Great Western and the Southern this was a privilege reserved for the first-class passenger. Many maintain that the LMS had the most comfortable carriages.

Punctuality was not a myth. The 'Big Four' all maintained a close watch on punctuality and competitions were held between regions or operating divisions to show who was best. Today, a train is only counted as being late if it is more than five minutes late, but between the wars a train was either on time or it was late, with no massaging of the figures. A minute late was a minute late. As for reliability, today train operators maintain that one failure for every 10,000 miles in service is good, but in 1946 the Great Western bemoaned the fact, as we will see later, that failures occurred, on average, every 40,000 miles owing to wartime neglect and post-war shortages, compared to once every 126,000 miles pre-war.

If you knew that you were travelling and expected to be away for some time, say a week or two, there was no need to struggle with your luggage. Not only did stations have porters with trolleys who would see you and your luggage between your taxi and the seat in your compartment, but you could also send your heavy luggage in advance so that it would be ready and waiting for you on arrival. The same could be done in reverse on the homeward journey. There were two rates for luggage in advance, the higher one being for door-to-door collection and delivery. A lower rate meant that your luggage would be collected from your home and await collection at your destination station or, as an alternative, it would be delivered to your destination address if you delivered it to your local station.

There were just two classes, first and third. This oddity had arisen because every railway had to provide third class for the so-called 'parliamentary trains', introduced in the nineteenth century to ensure a better deal for the poorest travellers. Second-class accommodation had started to disappear in the 1870s as the result of an initiative by the Midland Railway. This company, a predecessor of the LMS, overnight cancelled its second-class fares and started to scrap its small stock of third-class carriages, providing one of the biggest gains in the comfort of the third-class passenger. The Midland's action was not unconnected with its ambitions to operate from St Pancras to both Edinburgh and Glasgow, recognising that while its route was longer and slower than the west coast route from Euston and the east coast route from King's Cross, its carriages were more comfortable. With people paying third-class fares and travelling in what had been second-class carriages, they certainly were.

On the other hand, despite its extensive and expensive investment in electrification, speeds on the Southern Railway were well below the 60mph average. London to Brighton was conducted *non-stop* at an average speed just a shade over 50mph, while London to Portsmouth with three stops was at a speed of around 45mph. Nevertheless, the Southern was sufficiently aware of the impact of air transport that it had not only built a halt at Shoreham Airport, but a station for the original Gatwick Airport (the present airport is in a slightly different position), and with the Great Western Railway invested in Great Western & Southern Air Lines. The Southern also introduced trains designed to lure premium traffic away from the airlines. These trains included the all-Pullman 'Golden Arrow', which had its French counterpart, the

'*Flèche d'Or*', and its own all first-class ship, and the 'Night Ferry', a through sleeper train from London to Paris with wagons-lits sleeper stock scaled down to match the British loading gauge, which used the company's fleet of three train ferries.

On the 'Cornish Riviera', new rolling stock introduced in 1929 was replaced by even newer and better rolling stock in 1935. While the heavy investment in the best expresses had meant that good-quality rolling stock was 'cascaded' down onto lesser trains, not everything was as good as it might have been on some of the branch lines. True, it was probably better than the appallingly antique rolling stock on some French, Italian and Spanish branches, with wooden seats and with even main-line trains having leatherette seats and cramped compartments in third class, but on the LMS and LNER in particular, many branch-line trains were slow with dirty and antiquated rolling stock.

The years following the grouping saw the steady replacement of old four-wheeled rolling stock, and then it was the turn of the six-wheeled rolling stock, many of which ended their lives as 'camper coaches', self-catering accommodation located at stations that were either at beauty spots or close to them. On the LNER, Sir Nigel Gresley, the chief engineer, converted six-wheel carriages on suburban services to two-coach articulated sets, with a marked improvement in ride quality.

In one sense, however, railway carriage design was changing very slowly. Except for catering vehicles, most carriages featured doors that opened straight from compartments onto the platform. Shortly after grouping, the Great Western had produced corridor carriages without outside compartment doors, and found that these were unpopular with passengers. This could have been partly because the compartments still retained the three-window layout of the traditional compartment rather than the large single picture window that offered such fine views, or it could simply have been British conservatism manifesting itself. Passengers also objected to open saloon carriages at first, and it was not until the mid-1930s that the railway companies started producing carriages with large windows and without compartment doors, while open carriages were for the most part used for excursion trains. Even the Southern Railway's main-line electric multiple units only had open saloons with large windows in the driving coaches and catering vehicles.

On local and suburban services, the traditional compartment with doors did have two advantages. The first was that it offered a much higher seating capacity, while the second was that it ensured that passengers could alight or board very quickly, reducing station dwell times. Nevertheless, the London Underground used open carriages with sliding doors, except on the Metropolitan Line, where the rolling stock looked like main-line suburban stock with compartment doors. The LMS, however, did build new trains for its electrified lines on Merseyside with power-operated doors and open saloons with high-density seating.

Yet, only the Southern Railway and the Great Western showed real signs of using the new technology to improve the performance and appeal of their branch lines, despite the LMS having two third-rail networks, on Merseyside and from Euston to Watford, completed in 1924. On the Southern, everything was electrified to some 30 miles from the centre of London. Beyond that, electric trains worked passenger services on the electrified main lines to the Sussex coast and Portsmouth, including what might be described as 'secondary main lines', such as that to Alton, or the slow and relatively quiet route from Victoria to Portsmouth via Arundel, with a through average speed of around 35mph, or the coastal routes from Brighton to Portsmouth, or to Eastbourne and Hastings. However, there was still steam on many of the branch lines away from the London suburban area, such as those to Midhurst. The electric trains did in fact produce a significant improvement in the timings of stopping trains, where their superior acceleration showed them at their best.

The Great Western experimented with diesel railcars on the branch lines and the less busy main-line stopping trains, before developing what would today be described as a diesel multiple unit for a business express between Birmingham and Cardiff.

Despite the advantages of both diesel and electric traction being well known as early as the 1920s, there was no great haste to convert from steam. In 1939, Britain's railways were still mainly steam railways. Both the LMS and the GWR saw potential in diesel shunting locomotives, but both continued not only to build steam locomotives, but also to design and develop new and improved types. The Americans and Germans may have been introducing diesels, but in the UK coal was king. In some ways, this was to be a good thing, as in bankrupt post-war Britain the railways were at first encouraged to convert steam locomotives and their depots for oil firing, and then told to stop as the country no longer had the foreign exchange with which to import oil. Pre-war, the railways were able to pick and choose the coal they wanted, which meant that they got the best, and this was a factor in being able to obtain adequate performance from what were, in international terms, small steam locomotives. The pressures of war were to show that without the choice of the best coal, performance could suffer badly, especially on those locomotives with poor levels of superheating.

The adherence to steam contributed to the often dense winter fog that plagued operations, while the massive demand for coal meant that many lines were travelled by slow-moving, usually 'unfitted', that is to say unbraked, coal trains, often moving as little as 10mph. Except where lines had been quadrupled or provided with adequate passing loops, these hindered progress. Many of these trains were for the railways' own use, others were serving power stations and heavy industry, while many more were carrying household coal to the sidings that almost every station possessed in the days before these were turned into car parks.

Schoolchildren were taught in their geography classes that it was the freight trains, more popularly described as 'goods' trains, that made the money, but this was untrue. The railways with substantial passenger traffic were the more profitable. The railways were burdened by their obligations as a 'common carrier' to take anything that was offered, and rates for many types of traffic were uneconomically low. It may have been a good thing to keep much of this traffic off the roads, but it was the railways and their shareholders who bore the cost.

It should not be thought that the 'old' railways were simply plodding movers of coal, or perhaps coal and other mineral traffic. Their traditional traffics were widely varied in the days before road transport began to demonstrate its economy and flexibility and, one must say, security, as the shipper always knew where his consignment was using road haulage. Trains carried fresh fish from the many fishing ports, agricultural produce (with special trains for those items that were in season) and, of course, on a daily basis they carried milk. The Royal Mail had been carried on the railways from the early days, and on the longer-distance routes pre-war there were travelling post offices so that mail could be picked up automatically using special equipment by the lineside and deposited in the same way, with sorters working on the train so that the time spent on the rails was never wasted.

The railways were anxious to encourage new freight traffic, and even international freight traffic with the new train ferries. The growth in road transport did at least give the railways fuel to transport, and by the late 1930s six-wheeled tanker wagons were often to be seen alongside four-wheeled versions, while gas canisters were another traffic. Most significant were the special vans for transporting cars from the motor vehicle manufacturers' premises to distribution centres or the docks. In fact, loads of up to 120 tons could be carried by rail on special low-loader bogie wagons.

Of course, on the roads the railways had their customers' consignments to collect and deliver to and from the station. At the time of the grouping, most of this work used horse-drawn wagons. One improvement that did take place in the years leading up to the Second World War was that increasingly motor vans and lorries took over. The need to be able to operate in confined spaces meant that some ingenious solutions were tried and some proved enduring, such as the famous Scammell three-wheel tractor, the so-called 'Mechanical Horse', for articulated delivery vehicles.

The 'common carrier' obligation sometimes meant accepting traffic that was completely unsuited to the railways. If ships' lifeboats had to be delivered, these went by rail even if it meant that they had to be aligned on wagons so that they overhung on the 'off' rather than the 'near' side, where they might foul signals and trackside signs. Of course, overhanging on the offside meant that traffic on the other line had to be suspended while they travelled through. There were also many specials that must have been costly to organise and timetable, such as a special goods train to move an entire farm, or the trains taking a circus around the country. The former would require railway horse box wagons, cattle wagons and no doubt flat wagons for machinery and vans as well. The circus would need special wagons, including vans strengthened to take the weight of an elephant.

There were also many specials for passengers, with weekend summer holiday specials running between towns that did not normally have a through train service. Instead of jumping in the car or taking a seat on a motor coach for a day out at the seaside, excursion specials were laid on. These were made possible by keeping large quantities of rolling stock that was idle for most of the time. In some cases, elderly rolling stock was used, but the Great Western actually built new open saloon carriages for its excursion traffic. The 'Cornish Riviera' express was just one train throughout the year, but for an August Saturday sufficient rolling stock, including kitchen and dining cars, had to be rustled up to run it as four or five trains. On the Portsmouth line there was a single hourly fast train to and from Waterloo, except on summer Saturdays, when there were four an hour. The Southern did at least have trains that worked its weekday commuter traffic that could also be used for a summer Saturday extra, but the Great Western had not.

While attention centred on the high-stepping fast express locomotives, such as the 'Coronation' class of the LMS, the A4s of the LNER and the 'King' class of the GWR, the real success was the development of ever more capable mixed-traffic locomotives such as the LMS Stanier 4–6–0 'Black Fives' and the GWR 'Hall' class. These could attain speeds as high as 90mph, and were capable of handling the lighter expresses, suburban commuter trains or fast fully fitted goods trains. Such locomotives were built in their hundreds, while there were also the 2–8–0 and 0–6–0 goods locomotives for the many mineral and coal trains.

The railways were not completely blind to the need to enhance productivity. The LMS was keen on mechanical handling, while the GWR introduced small tractors to tow baggage trolleys on station platforms. The electric trains and diesel railcars needed just two men instead of the three needed by even a short steam train. There was also cooperation in such matters as selling freight to industrial and business customers, but it was to take the pressures of wartime and the need to economise on fuel for the railway companies to combine and coordinate their collection and delivery services.

Increasingly the railways dropped the idea of a steam locomotive being the preserve of a single crew or the same two crews if double shift working was in force, or even three crews for round-the-clock operation. Instead, locomotives were passed from one crew to another, and on a longer journey might have several crews, with men being changed at intervals to save the cost of having an overnight lodging while away from home. This cut costs, but it also meant that engine drivers and firemen were less aware of a locomotive's faults and less inclined to put themselves out to ensure that any defects were repaired. The old system had contributed greatly to reliability. The improved productivity of ending the link between a locomotive and one, two or even three crews, with driver and guard usually a semi-permanent team, may have come at a high cost, as the Great Western rejected the system and enjoyed the lowest locomotive operating costs of any of the 'Big Four'.

INTER-COMPANY COOPERATION

The coordination of the GWR and Southern Railway shipping services between the south coast of England and the Channel Islands was another means of improving the service to the customer, avoiding cut-throat competition that not only affected costs, but had also seen some risky ship handling by the more adventurous masters. The railways moved into air transport and at an early stage decided to do this collectively with Railway Air Services (RAS), before the Great Western and the Southern Railway decided that the other two companies were less ambitious in developing air transport than they were, so Great Western & Southern Air Lines was born. It might seem odd for the railways to embrace a competitive mode of transport, but both could see the potential for services to the Channel Islands and even the Isle of Wight, while Cardiff–Plymouth was a far easier journey by air than by railway. The Southern, with an eye on its lucrative cross-Channel traffic and aware of the inroads being made into its premium traffic by the airlines, even at one stage offered to buy the European services of Imperial Airways.

The railways did not operate in a vacuum. The 'Big Four' were independent of one another, but the passenger could buy a ticket from Wick to Penzance even before the grouping. This was owing to the work of the Railway Clearing House (RCH), which balanced receipts and payments between the companies for through traffic or for trains that operated over another company's lines. The RCH, based in London, did the same for freight consignments. It also worked to standardise such items as engine headcodes, although both the Southern and the Great Western also had their own additional codes to refine route identification further.

The railways also came together as members of the Railway Companies Association, which represented them politically and industrially. It was the Railway Companies Association that mounted the 'Square Deal' campaign on behalf of the 'Big Four'. They also collaborated in many marketing campaigns, such as one during the 1930s encouraging people to take their dog by train, and another for sending luggage in advance. Abroad, the railway companies operated as one, having a joint office in Paris and another in New York, and the latter saw one of the first uses of the title 'British Railways'.

The railways also cooperated when they acquired the nationwide road-haulage concerns Pickfords and Carter Patterson, buying these jointly. This also happened on occasion when they started buying into bus companies, with Devon General, for example, being owned jointly by the Great Western and the Southern, while Crossville was owned jointly by the Great Western and the London Midland & Scottish. The railways' bus services were amalgamated into the bus companies that they bought into, sometimes creating new companies. The old idea of the railway buses taking passengers to and from the trains was soon forgotten, and the companies even bought into the rapidly expanding long-distance coach services.

Occasionally, the investment in bus operation encouraged the railways to close hopelessly uneconomic branch lines, and sometimes a joint bus-train integrated service would be offered. Nevertheless, these ventures really were 'occasional', and bus-railway integration proved elusive, just as it did when the railways and most of the country's buses, apart from those in municipal ownership, were nationalised.

Despite their own financial difficulties, the reluctance of the four railway companies to close uneconomic branch lines was considerable. There were three railway lines into the small village of Midhurst in Sussex, from Petersfield, Pulborough and Chichester, and two into the small town of Peebles in the Scottish borders, from Edinburgh and from the west coast line. Many branch lines had just a handful of trains a day, often short trains of perhaps just a single carriage, and were completely incapable of ever covering their costs. The administrative difficulties in withdrawing railway services may have been one aspect of this, but it may also be that the 'Big Four' were more conscious of the economic benefit of these branch lines as feeders to the main lines and into the great expresses.

The railways were complete inter-modal transport operators, and had an astonishing degree of self-sufficiency. They built most of their locomotives and carriages. Both the London Passenger Transport Board and the Southern Railway had their own electricity generating stations, as did the Great Western for its depots and stations in the London area.

It was not enough to carry the traveller. It was also important that passengers could be accommodated on arrival, so the railways were the main owners and operators of many of the larger hotels. The LMS was not just the largest railway, it was also Britain's largest hotelier.

Of course, the other big difference between then and now was that the country had a thriving merchant fleet and this included a substantial number of vessels operating along the coasts. Even small ports were viable and would handle small vessels delivering coal or other bulk commodities. The railways served the small ports, but in wartime this heavy coastal trade was unable to travel along the east coast, and the traffic was instead handled by the railways.

Most of all, this was a railway with about twice the route mileage that it has today, with a total of 20,200 miles. Of this 20,200 miles, some 1,850 miles had three or more tracks – which usually meant four as a third or a fifth track was usually a relief close to a major terminus or junction – and another 10,800 miles was double track. The remainder, 7,550 miles, was single track and mainly consisted of branch lines, as there were very few through single-track lines, the Mid-Wales Line and the lines radiating out from Inverness being the notable exceptions.

CHAPTER 5

THE STORM CLOUDS GATHER

As the 1930s progressed, it became increasingly clear that a major European war was coming, and that once again it could be a global conflict. Attitudes to the threat of war had changed considerably over the decade. At the beginning of the 1930s, no one had wanted to believe that war would come again, and a Parliamentary by-election was lost by a candidate fighting on a re-armament ticket. Even late in the decade, politicians and public alike tried to pretend that peace could be saved, the former because the state of the economy meant that there was little money for warfare, and the latter because of the traumatic effect of the previous conflict, still known as the Great War, and often referred to as 'the war to end all wars'.

Today, with the 20:20 vision of hindsight, appeasement may have seemed pointless and even counter-productive, but at the time it was a popular policy. In its 1940 report on British attitudes to the Second World War, the newly created survey of public attitudes, Mass Observation, reported that: 'The leadership which found the prospect of peace in our time in a small piece of paper, was a leadership intensely acceptable to a nation which had made up its mind in 1918 not to fight another war if it could possibly be avoided.'

Naturally enough, the railways were no strangers to warfare. In addition to their own experiences in the United Kingdom during the First World War, many railwaymen had served abroad with the armed forces in Europe and in Mesopotamia – modern Iraq. Railway management also knew that any future war would be more difficult, more threatening, than the last, as they shared in the general consensus that 'the bomber would always get through'. Like most of the rest of the population, they had seen the cinema newsreel footage of the Spanish Civil War, of the Italian invasion of Abyssinia and the Japanese actions in China, all of which had emphasised the supremacy of the aeroplane.

For the railway companies, the coming conflict would be worse than the earlier war in other ways as well. The years preceding the First World

War had been ones of prosperity and progress, so when the government took control of the railways on the outbreak of war in 1914, compensation for their use had to be based on the average of the most recent peacetime years. Unfortunately, the years between the two world wars had been difficult ones for Britain's railways, already often referred to and even referring to themselves in their international marketing as 'British Railways'. When more than 120 companies, some of them very small and already operated by larger neighbours, were grouped into four big companies, strict control had been placed on fares and freight rates, and it was estimated that the railway companies should each achieve a 'standard revenue' each year, but these revenues, set in 1921 and 1922, were never achieved. It was clear that the level of compensation in any future state control would be based on some very lean years indeed. Even the Great Western, which had been the most consistently profitable railway between the wars, only managed to pay a dividend of half of 1 per cent for 1938, the first time in almost seventy years that the dividend had dropped below 3 per cent.

A POOR FINANCIAL OUTLOOK

That the railways eventually played such an important role so successfully once the Second World War started was by no means a happy accident. Nevertheless there was a sense of foreboding, especially among the railway company directors and the senior officers.

With their experience of the First World War recent enough still to be much to the fore as war loomed again in Europe, the directors of the railway companies were pessimistic about the prospects for their companies and their shareholders. In the earlier conflict, the fact that the railways had been guaranteed their 1913 revenues had been reassuring, for as explained earlier, this had been a good year. Not one of the years between the two wars had been nearly so good, and shareholders had had to accept scarce money being devoted to keeping the system up to date, and even extensively modernised, rather than being devoted to dividends. Given what has often been described as the 'short-termism' of the modern stock market, the railway directors and proprietors – the shareholders – had shown a remarkable degree of public spirit that would be hard to find today. Indeed, given their eventual reward, the fair minded can only say 'small wonder'. Even so, the financial situation of the railways had deteriorated miserably during the previous period of state control, largely because of a complete failure by the state to control costs. On grouping in 1923, the new companies inherited a backlog of maintenance and renewals left over from the war years.

Fresh concerns about war were coupled with the realisation that much would be different this time. It was realised that the railways would be prime targets for aerial bombardments in a way that had not happened on any great scale during the First World War.

Another big difference lay in the fact that before the earlier conflict, the railways had still been the supreme mover of goods and people inland, although this had been dented somewhat in the larger urban areas by the success of the electric tramways, especially where railways had been slow to electrify their suburban lines. Between the two wars, road transport had undermined the railways, almost entirely due to the spread of motor transport into road haulage, bus and coach services, for the private car was still a rarity. It was clear that wartime would be accompanied by stringent fuel rationing, and that much of the traffic carried by road would come back to the railways. This was not a matter for rejoicing, as the railways would be expected to take on the extra burden without having benefited from road-haulage revenues, or having to provide the resources, for some twenty years. Once again, we come back to the basis on which railway revenues would be protected.

PREPARING FOR WAR

Preparation for the wartime operation of the railways was put in hand as early as 1937. A Railway Technical Committee was formed with a brief to report on the steps that would need to be taken to protect the railways and ensure that traffic continued to move regardless of whatever enemy action might occur.

The main areas the committee had to look at included:

1. Protection of railway personnel.
2. Protection of key points, including administrative and control centres.
3. Provision of stocks of material for emergency repairs.
4. Provision of additional equipment.
5. Lighting restrictions.

The committee was probably hampered to some extent by its size, as it included representatives from the four grouped railway companies, the 'Big Four', from the London Passenger Transport Board, and representatives of both the Home Office and the Ministry of Transport. The committee was chaired by Michael (later Sir Michael) Barrington-Ward, the LNER's Southern Superintendent. He was joined by two other railwaymen, Gilbert Matthews of the Great Western and H.E.O. Wheeler of the Southern. The LMS representative was Capt J.O.N. Wood, whose role was to represent dock and shipping interests. Signalling and communications was also covered by the Great Western and the Southern, with F.H.D. Page and Col G.L. Hall respectively. As it was anticipated that the main weight of any air attack would fall on London, the London Passenger Transport Board was allowed to send a team of five representatives, headed by F.G. Maxwell. The Ministry of Transport was represented by two of its inspecting officers of railways, Sir Alan Mount and Col A.H.C. Trench, both former members of the Royal Engineers.

Nevertheless, despite the size of the committee, it worked with considerable urgency. While the Munich crisis was still some way off, the German annexation of Austria came early in 1938, causing alarm bells to ring. The committee's report appeared in June 1938, with an estimate of the costs of providing the level of protection recommended, which for the railway companies and London Transport came to £5,226,400, some £321 million today. This was a considerable sum for companies that were struggling to cover their costs and who were already aware that the improved earnings of 1937 were not being repeated in 1938. It was hoped that the government would be generous, not only in recognising the plight of the railways, but also in realising their importance to the country as a whole and to the war effort in particular. A foretaste of things to come followed when the government decided at the end of 1938 to provide a grant of just £4 million, of which £750,000 was to go to the LPTB, with the companies left to fund the balance themselves.

The GWR share of this reduced sum was £472,000, the lowest for any railway company, while the Southern Railway received only slightly more, £496,950, despite having no fewer than seven London termini and a substantial suburban network and, of course, being the railway that would handle most of the troop movements to the Continent. A much larger amount went to the LNER, £764,950, while the highest sum went to the LMS, the largest railway company, £1,359,700. This came to a total of £3,093,250, leaving the rest of the money to be spent on equipment that would be pooled between the four railway companies. Stores were built up of materials that would be necessary to maintain a railway under heavy aerial attack. For example, the civil engineers received an additional three months' supply of materials necessary to repair and maintain the permanent way, as well as timber baulks and strut joists. An additional three months' supply of locomotive and carriage spare parts was also ordered.

While the three-month reserve seemed adequate for most needs, the more complicated nature of the signal and telegraph stores and the longer lead times for replacement items, meant that in these cases a twelve-month reserve stock was regarded as being prudent.

RELOCATION

Part of the money was spent on relocating the headquarters of the four main-line companies, as it was vital that the railway continued to function no matter what happened. The main centre for the GWR became Beenham Grange, close to the station at Aldermaston in Berkshire. This was really not quite big enough, but additional buildings were found for some of the departments at Brimpton, Thatcham, Chosey and Reading. The Southern Railway evacuated as many of its staff as possible to the Deepdene Hotel near Dorking in Surrey, from where it was possible to reach both Waterloo and Victoria by train, but the general manager and his staff returned to Waterloo after six months, although as later experience was to prove, this was not a wise move. The LNER evacuated its chief general manager to The Hoo, a large country mansion near Hitchin, which officially became 'HQ1 Hitchin', but as a much larger railway it had to find many more centres for other departments and in fact these were more widely scattered than was the case even with the Great Western. Despite its size, the largest company, the LMS, had one of the more successful relocations, taking another country mansion, The Grove, near Watford, which had parkland stretching for 300 acres in which many departments could be located in temporary buildings.

As with any such move, the impact on the employees of the railway companies was considerable. While each company had moved away from London but had remained within its area of operations, the daily commute by staff was changed considerably and the new locations were far from convenient for those whose homes were based on a regular daily train journey to and from London. New travel arrangements had to be established with special trains in some cases, while overnight accommodation was included in the dispersal arrangements for those needing it. Canteen provision had been patchy in British industry generally before the Second World War, especially for office staff, but the new locations lacked the cafés and other catering facilities that staff had been accustomed to, so canteens also had to be established. In any case, plans for wartime rationing later assumed that workers would be fed at their place of work in the middle of their shift.

The moves affected large numbers – as many as 4,500 in the case of the LMS at Euston – but half of these were already in place after a frantic weekend effort before the outbreak of war on 3 September 1939.

The Railway Clearing House, which effectively made inter-company relationships and operations work, was moved out of London to Amersham.

THE RAILWAY EXECUTIVE COMMITTEE

As early as September 1938, the Ministry of Transport had warned that as soon as the danger of enemy aggression was imminent, a Defence of the Realm Act would be passed, and that one of its provisions would be for the government to take control of the railways and the railway operations of the London Passenger Transport Board. That same month, once again a Railway Executive Committee (REC) was formed. This was a different committee from that established in 1914. At that time there had been more than 120 railway companies, although some of them were operated by larger neighbouring companies, and no fewer than ten railways were represented on the First World War REC, with no representation at all for the London Underground lines. The Second World War REC was established early enough to have an advisory role while the companies remained in the hands of their managements, and all four main-line companies were represented along with the LPTB.

As the link between the railways and the government, the Railway Executive Committee was the one head office structure that could not be moved out of London. The members of the REC had to be close to government and the major service ministries – at that time each service had its own separate government department. As it happened, in a convenient location lay a disused deep-level Tube station, Down Street on the Piccadilly Line, that could be converted to become the wartime headquarters of the REC, complete with overnight accommodation and meeting facilities. Down Street was chosen in preference to a closed station, Museum, near the British Museum, on the Central Line, as a more convenient location. Had not Down Street been available, the Aldwych branch, also on the Piccadilly Line, could no doubt have been used as a less conveniently sited location, but as it was this was then available for other uses, as we will see later.

BLACKOUT

Despite the disruption caused by a serious signal-box fire at Paddington, preparations for wartime operations continued, and a trial blackout was tried at Paddington with a major air-raid precautions (ARP) exercise at the terminus between 1 a.m. and 4 a.m. on 29 January 1939.

This was all part of the rehearsal over the year or so before the outbreak of war. Railwaymen practised working in blackout conditions, which meant that no lights could be shown externally, with all windows screened, while station platforms could only be lit by blue lights or, as there were still many lit by gas, specially shaded gas lamps. Drivers had to pull up their trains beside oil lamps placed on the platform as markers. Steam locomotives had canvas draped between the engine cab and tender to hide the light of their fires, while the side windows on the more modern locomotives were blanked out. Colour light signals which had improved railway safety were now a danger because they were so visible from the air, and long hoods had to be fitted over them. At first trains ran at night without interior lights, but later shaded lights were introduced.

Such practices gave the train operators, and especially drivers and signalmen, serious problems, but these were almost as nothing compared with those suffered by the men working on track and signals. There were experiments to see if shaded lights could be used that could not be seen from the air.

After the outbreak of war, the realisation dawned that operating in the blackout posed many issues of efficiency and safety. The wartime blackout produced many minor accidents, with more than 230 occurring in the first two months of war at Paddington alone, mainly due to passengers stumbling or tripping in the dark. Work on the track was difficult, and so too was work in the marshalling yards, where the throughput of trains at night was down by some 10 per cent, even though traffic was growing under the pressures of wartime. Movement of goods trains at night kept the lines clear for faster passenger traffic during the day and, especially in the case of the fast freight trains, enabled shippers to deliver their goods at the end of the day for overnight delivery to their customers. Eventually, brighter lighting was permitted in the marshalling yards, although this was still far below that considered necessary for safe and efficient working in peacetime. The improved lighting was on condition that it would be cut immediately an air-raid warning was heard, and this meant re-wiring and having a man stationed permanently by the master light switch.

On the Great Western alone, no fewer than 136 goods stations and marshalling yards had to be re-wired. This was necessary because, by using aerial reconnaissance to test the effectiveness of the blackout, it had been shown that even with dimmed lighting, the glow of the marshalling yard lights could be seen for 15 miles by aircraft at 5,000ft.

Wartime acted as a spur to extending loudspeaker announcements to stations, and while initially station name signs were no longer lit, those under station canopies were allowed to be illuminated later provided that they were swung round at right angles to the platform. Lighting at stations was dimmed down and at many stations blue lights were used. Stations that had had their names painted on the canopies to help airmen with their navigation had them blanked out. Two final safety measures at stations were the removal of glass from roofs and canopies, essential since even a small bomb could create so many shards of broken glass as to be an effective anti-personnel weapon and, at major city stations, the preparation of air-raid shelters for the often large numbers of passengers who might be caught on an exposed platform or concourse during an air raid.

Air raid warning notices were posted on the inside of railway carriages. Just as householders were not allowed to show a light at night, railway carriages were also blacked out as far as possible. The usual practice, even on express trains, was to show nothing better than either a weak dimmed amber light or blue lighting. The exceptions were the Pullman carriages on the Southern Railway, which offered full lighting because they enjoyed a complete blackout in the form of wooden shutters that could be placed across the windows. This raised some objections in Parliament, but these were more political than practical. For the ordinary passenger, especially on a long journey, the poor lighting may have made them more secure, but it made reading difficult. The blackout at stations and the dim lighting within the carriages also made it difficult for passengers to identify their destination station. Later, improved lighting was introduced, especially on long-distance trains, but it remained a problem on branch-line and suburban trains which were constantly stopping with doors opening for passengers to board or alight. The ideal would have been something similar to the mechanism on modern cars that switches the interior light on when a door is opened, but working in reverse to switch off the lights whenever a door opened. Unfortunately, this would have been expensive and prohibitive in terms of the materials and manpower needed to convert many thousands of carriages with up to twenty doors each.

NATIONAL SERVICE

Meanwhile, many employees enrolled in the civil defence and air-raid precautions services, while others were already in the Territorial Army, many of them in the Railway Supplementary Reserve of the Royal Engineers, or were planning to join. Railway management could look forward to seeing many of the most experienced and most able men being taken away.

During the First World War, the railways had suffered due to the number of experienced and skilled men away on war service. The Second World War once again saw many senior railwaymen pressed into government service of one kind or another, of whom Gilbert Szlumper, the new general manager of the Southern Railway, was simply the most notable. On 26 May 1939, the Military Training Act was passed requiring all railwaymen between the ages of 20 and 21 years of age to register so that they were liable to be called up for military training. When war finally came, the National Service (Armed Forces) Act made every man, other than apprentices under the age of 21, between the ages of 18 and 41 years liable to be called up. The railway companies pressed for railwaymen to be exempted from the workings of both acts. The Minister of Labour did not feel that he could grant a blanket exemption, but as a compromise included railwaymen in a schedule of reserved occupations. The idea of the schedule was not to take men into the armed forces when their civilian role was vital to the war effort *and* their skill and experience would be of little value to the armed forces. This last clause was noteworthy since it meant that if the army required railwaymen to operate trains in a war zone, it could still have them.

The minister was also concerned to ensure that the railways were able to keep their experienced staff, but that inexperienced staff did not shelter behind the reserved occupation. So, minimum ages were applied below which the reserved occupation classification could not be applied. In most cases this minimum age was 25 years, with a higher minimum age of 30 years for a number of categories, such as permanent way staff, porters and goods checkers, unless they were in a supervisory role. This does seem to show that due recognition was given to the more skilled personnel.

The work of the Railway Technical Committee was only just in time, as it turned out. It is worth reflecting that, had the Munich Agreement of 4 October 1938 not been reached, few if any of the preparations recommended by the committee would have been put in hand, let alone implemented. Widely regarded even today as having been a disastrous mistake, there is little doubt that the Munich Agreement bought valuable extra time in which to put the country onto a war footing. The Minister of Transport would have had his Railway Executive Committee, and would have been able to take control of the railways, but the system would have lacked everything that would enable it to survive the heavy German bombing. It is also worth bearing in mind that the Royal Air Force in particular, in 1938, was still heavily dependent upon fighter designs that were obsolete, and lacked even a good medium bomber. The outcome of the Battle of Britain could well have been different if fought a year earlier, and the defences against the Blitz that much weaker. For a start, the 'Chain Home' radar network that did so much to foil German attacks and ensured that the small number of RAF fighters were always in the right place at the right time, would not have been completed.

CHAPTER 6

WHOSE RAILWAY IS IT?

True to its word, shortly before the outbreak of war the government moved to take control of the railways. One difference with the situation on the outbreak of the First World War was that instead of the President of the Board of Trade, the Railway Executive Committee came under the control of the Minister of Transport, which later, in 1940, became the Minister of War Transport. The then minister, Capt Euan Wallace, actually seized control of the railways on 1 September 1939, before the outbreak of war, using powers granted under the Defence Regulations Act 1939, with the Emergency (Railway Control) Order.

Once again the minister operated through a Railway Executive Committee, which had been formed the previous September, and included the general managers of the four main-line railways and London Transport. The London termini were obvious targets, so the railways had already evacuated many of their administrative personnel to the outskirts and to the provinces. The Railway Executive Committee itself found safety in an abandoned Underground station on the Piccadilly Line at Down Street, between Green Park and Hyde Park Corner stations, providing office accommodation and dormitories.

Initially, the Railway Executive Committee was chaired by Sir Ralph Wedgwood, who was chief general manager of the London & North Eastern Railway, but when he retired early in 1939, he was asked to remain as chairman of the REC rather than retiring from that automatically. His deputy as chairman was Sir James Milne of the Great Western Railway, while Wedgwood's successor at the LNER also became a member of the REC. The other members were Sir William Wood of the London Midland & Scottish and Mr Gilbert Szlumper of the Southern Railway, with Mr Frank Pick of the London Passenger Transport Board. The REC secretary was Mr G. Cole Deacon from the Railway Companies Association. Later, when Szlumper was transferred to the War Office as Director-General of Transportation (*sic*), his place both as general manager at Waterloo and on the REC was taken by Eustace Missenden.

The REC worked through a series of section sub-committees which were, for the most part, based on the structure of the Railway Clearing

House with its sub-divisions. There were a few additional sub-committees, however, including one set up to prepare for sabotage. In all, there were sixteen sub-committees, and pulling their work together must have been a challenge. As it happened, sabotage was not a major problem and was more likely to come from members of the Irish Republican Army than from any German agents.

COMPENSATION AND CONTROL

Meanwhile, the shareholders were still waiting to learn what compensation they would receive for what effectively amounted to the requisition of their property. The haste to grab control of the railways was in contrast to the tardiness in finalising the arrangements. In 1914, agreement had been reached quickly, in September, using the Regulation of the Forces Act 1871, but in 1939, using the new Emergency Powers (Defence) Act 1939, the government was dragging its feet. Encouraged by the delay in reaching agreement, the Labour MP for Bristol South asked the Minister for Transport, on 22 November, if he would consider nationalising the railways. The minister rejected this at the time, assuring the House that he was confident that agreement would be reached shortly, and also reminding them that unified control had already been achieved through the Railway Executive Committee. Another month passed, and the question of nationalisation was becoming more serious, as rumours that it was being considered (that could only have been officially inspired) began to circulate, obviously intended to apply pressure to the railway companies.

'It cannot be for the good of the community that such a monopoly as a main line should be controlled by any group of individuals, however public spirited,' ran one statement on the matter, completely ignoring the fact that the railways were no longer controlled by the companies, but instead by the REC. Many writers on railway matters saw opportunism in these threats, arguing that those in favour of nationalisation would find their arguments less convincing in a period when policy could be considered at leisure. Even so, it was not until 7 February 1940 that the minister was able to give the House of Commons the news that agreement had been reached.

State control made the railways contractors to the government. All revenue passed to the government, which then allocated shares from a pool, initially set at a guaranteed £40 million (around £2,152 million today). The Southern share of the pool was fixed at 16 per cent, the same as for the GWR, while the LPTB received 11 per cent, the LMS 34 per cent and the LNER 23 per cent. These percentages were based on the average net revenues for the companies and LPTB in the three years 1935–7, which the government took as each company's standard revenue. Once the guaranteed £40 million had been paid, any balance was allocated to the five train operators on the same percentage terms up to a maximum of £3.5 million. After this, if there was a further balance, the revenue over £43.5 million would be divided equally between the government and the pool until the pool total reached £56 million. At this stage, if the revenue share allocated to any of the companies then exceeded its standard revenue, the excess would be shared out proportionately among the other companies.

Costs of maintenance and renewals had to be standardised, while the cost of restoring war damage would be met up to a total of £10 million in a full year. Privately owned wagons were also requisitioned by the Ministry of War Transport, and the individual companies had to meet the costs and revenue attributable to the wagon owners out of their share of the revenue pool. The importance of the private owner wagons to rail freight can be gathered from the fact that in 1939 there were 652,000 wagons owned by the grouped companies, and another 585,000 wagons in private ownership, of which the collieries and coal merchants had the greatest number.

This was a 'take it or leave it' type of agreement, with the government leaking threats of nationalisation if the companies failed to agree, although these were officially denied. While the years in question had been bad ones for the British economy, the final year, 1938, had been even worse and the railways had had great difficulty in getting the government to understand this. The railway companies never achieved the revenues anticipated by the Railways Act 1921. All that can be said for the deal was that the government was anxious to avoid inflationary pay claims from railway employees, but the inescapable fact was that the railways were having their revenues more or less fixed while costs were bound to rise as they struggled to meet the increased demands that wartime would place upon them. The upper limit on the costs of war damage was either political expediency to keep the unions quiet and retain the Labour Party in the wartime coalition government, or simple naivety since normal insurance measures were not available in wartime.

In addition to taking over the 'Big Four' and London Transport, the Emergency (Railway Control) Order also applied to joint committees of any two or more of these railways, and to other lines, including the East Kent, Kent & East Sussex, and Shropshire & Montgomery light railways, the King's Lynn Docks & Railway and the Mersey Railway. Anyone who has regarded the Romney Hythe & Dymchurch Railway as a 'toy railway', with its 15-in gauge and scaled-down locomotives based on standard-gauge designs, should know that this was requisitioned by the military, becoming a vital link in the defences of a low-lying, and therefore vulnerable to invasion, section of the Kent coast. The government had earlier warned the railways that as many as 800 locomotives might be required for service overseas, but as the war did not follow the pattern of 1914–18, not all were required.

While the railways were expected to give up manpower and equipment for the armed forces, the impact was less than during the First World War, in which 184,475 men were conscripted. Some 110,000 men had to be given up for national service, with more than 100,000 actually conscripted into the armed forces, while 298 steam locomotives and forty-five of the still-rare diesel locomotives, all of them shunting engines, were also taken for service overseas. These figures were in addition to the use of railway workshops for war work, which naturally moved a further substantial number of personnel away from railway work.

Once the Soviet Union entered the war after the German invasion of 1942, it sought supplies from both the United Kingdom and the United States. While most of the supplies from the UK went on the famous Russian Convoys to Murmansk and Archangel, most of the American supplies entered the USSR from the south, through Persia, as Iran was then known. The Persian railway system was initially not up to the task, and needed additional locomotives and rolling stock. The system had many steep gradients, and the War Office requisitioned forty-three Stanier 2–8–0 locomotives from the LMS, and from the LNER ninety-two of the 2–8–0 Class 4 locomotives inherited from the Great Central Railway.

The financial basis of state control of the railways in wartime had been agreed or, depending on one's viewpoint, imposed. Nevertheless, it was soon clear that the original scheme had many deficiencies, and as early as December 1940 a short Act of Parliament allowed those railways under the control of the Minister of Transport to make agreements with the minister to cover financial matters arising from the period of control.

The railway companies were given the freedom to enter into arrangements, provided that the minister laid an order. In fact, the position of Minister of Transport had fallen prey to revolving-door syndrome, with the ailing Capt Euan Wallace replaced by Sir John Reith when Winston Churchill took over as prime minister. Reith was famous for having been the first director-general of the British Broadcasting Corporation (BBC). No great expert on railways, he was replaced in turn by Lt-Col J.T.C. Moore-Brabazon before the end of 1940, who lasted just six months or so before the Ministry became the Ministry of War Transport in May 1941 under Lord Leathers of Purfleet, and the 'new' department also absorbed the Ministry of Shipping. These changes meant that transport was in turn looked after by a man, although originally a civil engineer, whose reputation was based on creating the British Broadcasting Corporation, then it passed to one of the pioneers of aviation, and finally, in May 1941, to Lord Leathers, a businessman with extensive interests in coal, who was ennobled for the purpose rather than have the government wait for a Parliamentary by-election. Nevertheless, Lord Leathers' suitability for his new role was being questioned by the railway press as further negotiations between the railways and the Treasury were in hand. The fear was that the pursuit of the public interest would become too one-sided.

Part of the problem was that no one in government really understood, or perhaps even cared about, the problems encountered by the pre-war railways, let alone the difficulties facing them in this new conflict. As before, coastal shipping was badly affected by wartime conditions, but the seriousness of the situation was far worse than during the First World War. By mid-1940, German forces controlled Europe from the North Cape almost to Bordeaux, and occupied the Channel Islands. The North Sea and the English Channel were effectively out of bounds to merchant shipping, regardless of the strength of the convoys, although further west, shipments of Welsh coal to the south coast ports, including railway-owned Southampton, had more than trebled.

The Treasury was its usual unsympathetic and unrealistic self. The Chancellor of the Exchequer, Sir Kingsley Wood, decided that war damage would not be treated as an element within working expenses, which could be offset against the guaranteed sums paid by the government, but instead was to be charged to the capital account, transferring these uninsurable costs from the government to the railways. On 7 April 1941, in his Budget speech, the chancellor announced that the government's policy was to combat inflation and restrict price increases as far as possible, and that included railway fares and rates for goods traffic. This was important news, but it took more than a week for Moore-Brabazon to write to Lord Stamp of the LMS, the chairman of the Railway Companies Association. Unfortunately Stamp was killed that night, 16 April, in an air raid.

Moore-Brabazon moved on, so it was left to his successor, Lord Leathers, to explain to the railway companies the bad news about pricing and war damage, and even then, June 1941, the advice was oral, almost as if the government was ashamed to commit itself to paper. Instead of the original agreement of a £40 million guarantee and a share in net revenue in excess of that amount up to £56 million, there would be a fixed annual guarantee. The railway companies were in an impossible situation, with the nation expecting German invasion after having come through the Blitz. No one was to know at the time that salvation would come, in the short term, through the diversion of German attention to the invasion of the Soviet Union. To argue would be construed as being unpatriotic, and many would have had memories of how war profiteers had been vilified by the press and politicians in the First World War, although no one had ever suggested that such charges applied to the railways. The railway companies were negotiating under duress, and the government had clearly already settled on the fixed figure of £43 million, eventually referring to the changes in the light of the previous year's legislation permitting an amendment. The government promised to make good any deficiency in the fixed figure, but would also take any surplus.

Division of the £43 million and the relative shares were as follows:

Great Western	£6,670,603	15.5 per cent
Southern	£6,607,639	15.4 per cent
London Midland & Scottish	£14,749,698	34.3 per cent
London & North Eastern	£10,136,355	23.6 per cent
London Transport	£4,835,705	11.2 per cent

Clearly, there were winners and losers, although the variation in percentage terms was marginal. The Southern and Great Western were both slightly worse off in percentage terms, the former the more so, while the LMS, LNER and LPTB all made marginal gains. Shareholder protests that the deal was mean in the extreme were countered by socialists claiming that the deal was far too generous. The *Railway Gazette* reported:

Certain sections of the community, always vocal in these matters, have not disguised their disappointment that the Government has decided not to adopt the advice they have given so freely and with so little practical knowledge, to nationalise the transport system of the country. The new agreement, which provides for renting the railways by the State, has also been criticised on the grounds that its terms are unduly generous to the transport system. How little substance there is in these protestations is easy to see if one is prepared to delve far enough into the facts of the case, to divest one's mind of prejudice, and to approach the problem from the basis of equity. On this basis, the original agreement can by no means be judged generous to the proprietors of the railways; nor can the second. At best it provides a very meagre return upon the capital which has been invested in the undertakings and without which, allied to the patience which, perforce, has been exercised by a long-suffering body of stock-holders, the railways of this country could not have reached their present high standard of efficiency, which has contributed so greatly to the successful prosecution of the war.

Of recent years there has been all too prevalent an idea that the standard revenue which was fixed by the Railways Act, 1921, as fair and reasonable and in the public interest is beyond the possibility of attainment – that the £51,359,000 at which it now stands has become but a mythical figure. It should be remembered that Parliament considered the attainment of that standard revenue was so expedient in the public interest that it placed a duty on the Railway Rates Tribunal to fix charges so as to enable a company to earn its standard revenue. Although it is a fact that Parliament's object was not attained . . . this has been due very largely to acute and unregulated competition by road interests. There can be no doubt that in present circumstances the railway companies could earn their standard revenues. . . . Moreover, the use now made of the capital provided by the railways is much greater than in the period before the war, and includes the use of assets that were then operated at a loss, but were continued in use to meet conditions which now exist. Taking into consideration . . . the London Passenger Transport Board, a total of £56,853,000 would be required as the total standard revenue of the whole of the undertakings, and it is this figure that should be borne in mind when comparisons are made with the fixed annual revenue of the five major parties in the revised arrangements which provide for a rental of £43,000,000 in addition to the net revenue from certain excluded items.

The excluded items were the railways' revenue from associated businesses such as road haulage and bus operations. The *Railway Gazette* continued to emphasise that the railways had made considerable sacrifices in accepting the deal, but were obviously influenced by two factors: the national interest; and that while the earnings even for 1941 were far in excess of the sums provided by the deal, there could be developments that would reverse this situation, such as invasion. It went on to remind its readers that the railways would now have to pay for restoring their own war damage, and that there could be no grounds for suggesting that the £43 million annually was a subsidy to the railways. Instead it was clear that the railways were subsidising the government. Gross expenditure by the five railway undertakings controlled by the REC during 1940 had amounted to £203.5 million, of which more than £150 million was accounted for by labour costs, while the capital cost of the five undertakings amounted to £130 million. The £43 million included the revenue from ancillary businesses, and amounted to a return of less than 3.5 per cent on the capital. The one item that the railways could charge for was the manufacturing work carried out in railway workshops, which over the war totalled £38,999,000.

Further adjustments were not made in the later stages of the war when it was clear that the invasion threat was long past, even though the net earnings of the railways were by this time well in excess of their fixed annual payments by upwards of 100 per cent for three years running. In fact, the surplus profits taken by the government for 1943, 1944 and 1945 reached a total of £155 million. By this time, the railways were not simply serving the British armed forces, but in addition were playing their part in supporting the build-up of men and equipment for the invasion of Europe. There were also the leave specials not just for British servicemen who wanted to get home to see their families, but for Americans whose idea of a good time off-duty meant heading for London.

While in theory the railways could keep the money earned by their investment in road haulage and bus companies in the pre-war years, these were also constrained by the requisitioning of their property by the military, while buses, for example, could be directed from one company to another, as demand fluctuated. Companies in what had been, pre-war, holiday areas, suddenly found themselves with large military training camps and other bases to serve. They might be expected to provide vehicles without notice for troop movements, and this was especially the case for those in what would be regarded as 'invasion areas', such as the Isle of Wight, for example. Road transport was also constrained by its fuel supply, which on the outbreak of war was cut by 20 per cent, and later controlled thoroughly. Many bus operators experimented with low-pressure gas, towing trailers behind double-decker buses and sometimes putting gas bags on top of single-decker buses, but this was generally unsatisfactory. It was, in any case, easier to convert the petrol-engined vehicles than those with the increasingly common diesel engine, and when gas was used it was given to the petrol-engined vehicles.

CHAPTER 7

EVACUATION UPON EVACUATION

The outbreak of war was contemplated with much concern by those who had been observing world events during the 1930s. While the British and French governments had presented the Germans with an ultimatum, it was not known whether there would be a pre-emptive strike, with the Germans attacking without warning. It was for this reason that the government put its evacuation plans into action several days before war was expected.

Many believed that Germany must know that the British and French ultimatum over Poland would be followed by intervention, but this was to ignore the impression that the Munich Agreement the previous October had made on the Germans. In the United Kingdom, people feared a surprise attack by the Luftwaffe, a pre-emptive strike without any declaration of war. In fact, many in the German armed forces did not believe that war would break out with Britain and France before 1944 or 1945. It was also the case that German strategy during the first two years of war was to concentrate on one front at a time, and it was the abandonment of this policy with the attack on the Soviet Union in 1941 that marked a major turning point in the war.

INDUSTRIAL RELATIONS

Meanwhile, while so many were worried about the outbreak of war and its timing, the railways and the government faced another problem. The threat of war had not changed the turbulent nature of the British industrial relations scene. The period between the two world wars had been one of stable prices, indeed of deflation, and the railways had ensured that track and rolling stock were kept in good condition, and wherever possible modernised and improved, hoping for an eventual upturn in the economy to bring its rewards. All of this was done at the expense of paying dividends to the shareholders, many of whom were not necessarily wealthy, and some of whom may well have inherited their stock. There was little money to meet improved pay awards, although there were some changes to conditions of service, including shorter hours, much to the dismay of at least one general manager who argued that applying the same hours to the signalman or crossing keeper on a quiet country branch as to their counterparts on a busy main line was nonsense.

As war loomed, the vastly increased defence budget, with an all-out arms race that threatened to bankrupt the country, resulted in improved traffic, although not it seems improved profits, in 1938. The railway unions noted the improved traffic, which while still under their own managements meant greater prosperity for the railway companies, and started to agitate for a pay increase. It seems that the unions were also spurred on by Nazi propaganda that mocked the conditions for British workers, since this seems to have upset the then general secretary of the National Union of Railwaymen when addressing his audience at the NUR's AGM at Abergavenny in mid-August 1939. The result was a pay claim demanding a weekly minimum of £2 10*s* (around £134.50 today) for adults, to which the railway companies responded with an offer of £2 5*s*. For the sake of comparison, the best-paid skilled workers at this time earned about £3 10*s* per week, and the sums mentioned for railway workers would have been for unskilled staff. A new recruit to the armed forces would have received just 14*s* per week, and a corporal would have earned between £1 and £1 5*s* a week, although accommodation and food would have been provided free, and for married servicemen there would have been an additional allowance.

In the resulting impasse between the railway companies, the NUR decided to put its claim to the Railway Staff National Tribunal, but the Associated Society of Locomotive Engineers & Firemen (ASLEF) opted instead to bring out its members on strike from midnight on Saturday 26 August. Not all footplate staff belonged to ASLEF, but they were the overwhelming majority. Footplatemen were not the lowest paid, as engine drivers were a grade up from the most senior firemen, and they in turn were some steps above the cleaners and fire-setters in the engine sheds and depots.

The strike decision appalled politicians and the media. Ernest Brown, the Minister of Labour, met the ASLEF executive on 24 August, and at first the two sides went through a ritual recital of the basis of the claim, but then the Minister played his strong hand, emphasising that with war almost certain and evacuation plans already laid: 'We may need you to get the children away to safety.' This struck a chord, and later that day ASLEF called off the strike and agreed to follow the NUR in referring the claim to the Railway Staff National Tribunal. This was just as well, with the evacuation starting on 1 September, and the numbers involved were far beyond the abilities of any other form of public transport. Road vehicles were smaller then than today, and at the time a typical single-decker bus would have carried no more than thirty-five passengers, and a double-decker bus on two axles, as most motorbuses were, fifty-two or fifty-six. Trolleybuses could carry up to seventy passengers, but could not venture beyond the limits of their urban systems and were not present in every town or city. Trams were even more limited and inflexible.

The pay claim was based on a working day at a time when most public transport workers worked a six-day week. The difference between ASLEF members and those of the NUR showed in the claim, with the latter seeking the £2 10s minimum, while ASLEF looked for a £2 14s minimum for engine cleaners over the age of 22, plus the guarantee of a fireman's minimum rate and uniform if such a cleaner was not promoted to fireman after 313 firing turns. The minimum rate claimed for a fireman was £3 3s per week, rising to £3 12s with the guarantee of the driver's minimum, again after 313 driving turns (no doubt this somewhat peculiar figure was based on the number of shifts that could be worked in a year). For drivers and motormen, a minimum of £3 18s was sought, rising to £4 16s. These claimed rates were augmented by extra payments for Sunday working, amounting in theory to time and a half, but boosted further by the claim demanding an eight-hour minimum both for Sunday working and any roster that extended from Sunday into Monday. Two weeks, that is twelve working days, annual paid holiday was also demanded. The Railway Clerks Association also made a claim, largely along the lines of the other unions but with the additional claim that continuous night duty should attract one night in ten off in addition to normal rest days.

In total, the unions' claims amounted to an extra £4.8 million annually for the railway companies, at a time when their income was fixed by the government. The country went to war while the claims were being pursued. The Tribunal reported on them in late October, and succeeded in recommending a compromise that would increase the wage costs of the railway companies by £1 million. Minimum rates were raised to £2 7s for railwaymen in rural areas, with an extra shilling for those in industrialised areas, while those in London were to receive the £2 10s demanded by the NUR. A sign of the times was that women were to be paid around 12*s* (60p) less than men, and possibly the substitution of female labour for male as men joined the armed forces eased the burden on the railway companies. The Railway Companies' Association representative, Mr H.E. Parkes, produced a minority report proposing a lower settlement, generally some 2*s* less for adult males, but he accepted the Tribunal recommendations for women's pay. There were also some changes to minimum payments so that any Sunday roster would attract a minimum of four hours' pay for shifts of up to three hours, and for longer shifts, or if there were two short shifts, eight hours' pay would be given, but footplatemen were granted their Sunday claim of a minimum of eight hours' pay.

The unions accepted the offer, but by 1 December the NUR was back for more, asking the Railway Executive Committee for an all-round 10*s* a week cost-of-living increase. It is true that prices were beginning to rise and this was later to be a factor in the introduction of rationing, but for those on the minimum adult wage for the London area, this represented a pay increase of at least 20 per cent, and even more for those in the provinces and for women.

EVACUATION

For the first time the railways had to participate in a massive evacuation programme, moving children and expectant and nursing mothers away from areas judged to be at risk from enemy bombing. Evacuation was to be a problem that recurred during the war. Many first-wave evacuees drifted back home during the long months of the so-called 'Phoney War', the period between the outbreak of war and the start of the German advance, first northwards into Denmark and Norway and then westwards through the Low Countries and into France. As France fell, a further evacuation moved many evacuees away from what had now become an endangered zone, the coastal and country districts in the south-east and south of England as far west as Southampton, as well as evacuating many of the residents of those areas. A further evacuation later in the war was caused as the V-weapons took their toll on London and the south-east.

When evacuation was ordered on 31 August 1939, it was able to start the following day as plans had already been made by the railway companies. After the false hopes raised by the resolution of the Munich Crisis of 1938, it had soon become clear that war was more of a probability than a possibility. On 1 September, virtually the eve of war, the evacuation started of children and many others, including their teachers and expectant and nursing mothers, to get them away from London and the other major cities, especially those judged to be likely targets. The pressure on the Southern and other railways was such that during the four days of the operation, from 1 to 4 September 1939, only a skeleton service could be provided for the public outside the rush hours. As a typical example, while the Great Western ran a train from its evacuation station at Ealing Broadway every ten minutes, its main-line services were reduced to just eighteen trains from Paddington between 8.40 a.m. and 6.35 p.m. Those to the West Country were routed the 'long way round' via Bristol. Many goods trains were stopped during the period of the evacuation, with few, if any, running on 1 and 2 September.

In London alone, 5,895 buses were required to move 345,812 passengers to the suburban stations chosen as the entrainment points. The first evacuation special left Ealing Broadway on the Great Western Railway at 8.30 a.m. on Friday 1 September. All four railway companies handled this traffic. Not every parent sent their child away, and some made their own arrangements. Meanwhile, the railways were running evacuation specials in and around the main industrial conurbations and other likely target areas, such as Glasgow, Merseyside, Manchester, Tyneside, Birmingham, Portsmouth and Southampton.

The railways also had to arrange thirty-four ambulance trains for the partial evacuation of hospitals in these areas, while later all hospitals within 20 miles of the south coast were also partially evacuated. These measures were not just to move patients to places of greater safety, but to free beds for the bombing when it came, and also to empty hospitals near the coast in case of an invasion.

Many of the capital's evacuees must have made their own way to the departure stations or been taken on the Underground, as the total carried by the railways from London was 617,480, using 1,577 trains. While London had the biggest evacuation, many were being moved from other major industrial areas. After London, Merseyside had the next biggest evacuation, with 161,879 evacuees in 382 trains. Clydebank and Glasgow accounted for 123,639 evacuees with 322 trains, followed by Manchester with 115,779 evacuees and 302 trains. Nowhere else provided more than 100,000 evacuees, with a big drop between the Manchester total and that for Tyneside, where 73,916 evacuees were spread over 271 trains. Even Birmingham only provided the surprisingly low figure of

46,934 evacuees and 170 trains. Most of the evacuation trains seemed to have an average of around 400–500 passengers, but the two trains run from Rosyth on the Firth of Forth must have been very crowded, with a total of 2,187 evacuees between them. Despite their proximity to the Continent and the importance of the naval base, the Medway towns provided just 9,754 evacuees for fifty-four trains, and Portsmouth, a naval base, and Southampton, a major port, provided 36,917 between them for 172 trains.

Meanwhile, in addition to handling the evacuation, between 1 and 3 September, twenty-two special trains conveyed around 10,000 service personnel to the King George V Dock in Glasgow for passage to the Mediterranean, where they were to reinforce the garrisons, mainly in Gibraltar, Malta, Cyprus and Alexandria. Civilians were also reporting to labour exchanges as they received their call-up papers, meaning that there was yet more travel, albeit most of it over short distances. The achievement becomes still more incredible when it is also borne in mind that, during the evacuation and after it ended, 158,000 men were conveyed to the Channel ports and across the Channel to France, along with more than 25,000 vehicles, over a period of five weeks.

The problem was, of course, that at this early stage of the war, no one knew just how the situation would develop. The fall of France was not anticipated, nor was the earlier invasion of Denmark and Norway or the Netherlands. This was because most members of the military believed that there would be a re-run of the First World War with major fighting for the duration of hostilities on French or Belgian soil. The additional feature was to be heavy bombing, but only of those cities within range of German airfields. Plymouth, which was to suffer badly from the attentions of the Luftwaffe, was seen as being 'safe'. In fact, a further evacuation was to be necessary, but that would overlap with the evacuation of British forces from Dunkirk, and in the meantime, as the period of the 'Phoney War' continued through the winter of 1939–40, many evacuees drifted homewards.

NATURE TAKES A HAND

The evacuation of children and the immediate mass movement to France of the men of the British Expeditionary Force and the Advanced Air Striking Force were all over, fortunately, when nature took a hand. The line between Folkestone and Dover was known to be vulnerable to sudden falls of chalk. After a period of exceptionally high rainfall, on 27 November 1939, there was a fall of around 50 tons of chalk, which did not block the railway line, but alerted the Southern Railway to the possibility of further falls. Watchmen were posted around the clock in case of further falls. On 28 November, at around 6.55 p.m., the signalman on duty in the signal-box at Shakespeare Halt thought that he heard another fall of chalk, and a watchman was sent to investigate. In the darkness it was difficult to be sure of what had happened, and for safety's sake the signalman decided to stop all trains, and the 'Obstruction – Danger' signal was sent to Abbotscliff box to the west and Archcliffe Junction to the east. The next train was the 5 p.m. from Cannon Street to Dover, and the prompt action by the signalman meant that this train was stopped at Folkestone. Whether or not there had been a fall was immaterial, for shortly after the obstruction signal was sent, some 25,000 cubic yards of chalk descended on the line, tearing up the permanent way and sweeping all before it into the sea. There was a very real danger that the train could either have been caught by the landslide or run into it before it could stop.

Clearing this mess was no easy task. The approaches through the Shakespeare's Cliff Tunnel with its two tight single bores limited the equipment that could get to the site, and the tunnels were the only access. Worse, the entire cliff face was unstable, and before any work could start, the face had to be blasted back to a stable base. In the blackout, night work was impossible, and the daylight hours in winter were short. Much of the original fall was in blocks as heavy as 10 tons, and these had to be cut down to a manageable size by blasting before the earthmoving equipment could get to work. Nevertheless, the chalk covering the track was pushed into the sea to provide a breakwater that would stop the track being undercut, and it was little short of incredible that the line was reopened on 7 January 1940, only to be closed again by a further fall of chalk the following month.

It was instances like this that showed that the way in which the railway system had been created piecemeal was in fact a strength. While services between Folkestone and Dover were disrupted, and passengers had to be sent by bus, the through passengers travelled on trains that were diverted via Canterbury or Chatham.

The period immediately after Christmas 1939 saw the start of what was described by one railway house magazine as 'The worst winter in living memory.' It was made worse by the fact that services were already limited, and with fewer trains being run, there was not the frequent passage of trains and movement of signals and points that might help to stop the system icing up. The severe winter weather lasted from late December 1939 and through all of January 1940. The Southern Railway's electrified lines were especially badly hit as conductor rails froze. With the bad weather having started on a Sunday, when only a limited service was operating, many trains were trapped in the sidings. Communications were further disrupted as telegraph wires were brought down. On the more exposed electrified routes, steam locomotives had to assist the electric multiple units through the worst-affected lengths of track. Not that steam power was a solution in itself, as further north, on the London Midland & Scottish, many trains were trapped in snow drifts. Throughout most of the country, railway passengers suffered the worst disruption many had seen. Despite these problems, between 7 January and 7 February, a further substantial contingent of the BEF was moved to the Channel coast and then to France.

DUNKIRK

The 1940 Whitsun holiday was cancelled by the government since the Germans were sweeping through the Low Countries and into France. This ultimately led to the evacuation of the British Expeditionary Force from Dunkirk, along with many French troops and some from Belgium as well.

By the time of Dunkirk, six of the Southern Railway's cross-Channel packets and the Channel Island ferry *Isle of Guernsey* were working as hospital ships, while another eight, including *Autocarrier* and *Canterbury*, had been taken up from trade and were in service as military transports. Early on 29 May, the *Brittany* was also requisitioned by the government and warning was given that two more ships might be wanted, but by noon the situation was such that the signal was received that 'all available Southern Railway steamers of 1,000 tons gross with a range of 150 miles are required for immediate Government service'. Nine ships were quickly handed over, including four Isle of Wight ferries, of which two were car ferries with low open vehicle decks and certainly not best suited to a squall on the English Channel.

The Southern had already lost two ships by this time. On 23 May, the *Maid of Kent*, clearly marked as a hospital ship and crowded with wounded soldiers, sank in the harbour at Dieppe after being hit by five bombs. That same day, *Brighton*, again marked as a hospital ship, was also bombed and sunk.

On 30 May, *Lorina* and *Normannia*, operating as military transports, were both sunk at Dunkirk, although the crew of the latter were all saved and reached England. Another hospital ship, the *Paris*, was bombed on 2 June and the damage was such that she had to be abandoned. It was the small Isle of Wight paddle steamer *Whippingham* that took the record for the number of men rescued from Dunkirk, carrying 2,700 men on 4 June.

During the rest of the war, another seven Southern Railway vessels were lost to enemy action. The ships did not simply operate as military transports; some of the Isle of Wight paddle steamers served as minesweepers, although their work was usually close to home in the Solent.

Meanwhile, for the evacuation of the BEF from Dunkirk, four large GWR steamers had been employed in bringing troops back across the Channel. These were the *St Helier* and the *St Julien* from the Channel Island service, accompanied by the *St Andrew* and the *St David* from the Fishguard–Rosslare service. *St Andrew* and *St Julien* had already been operating as hospital ships. The *St Helier* alone carried no fewer than 10,000 troops across the Channel. These vessels were at the smart end of the operation, but the less fortunate troops found themselves on two of the Channel Island cargo steamers, the *Roebuck* and the *Sambur*. Their smaller size meant that these ships could go closer in at Dunkirk. Afterwards they were sent to St Valery to rescue troops from there, but by the time they arrived it was too late, as the port had fallen to the Germans. When the ships arrived, the Germans had shore batteries ready and a number of those aboard were killed as the ships came under fire. Too late for the Dunkirk evacuation, but a sign of the desperation felt at the time, was the *Mew*, the Dartmouth–Kingswear ferry, which also answered the call, but by the time she reached Dover the evacuation was ending.

The *St Andrew*, *St David* and *St Julien* were later sent to the Mediterranean, and instead of taking troops off beaches, played an important part in the invasion of Sicily and later at the Salerno landings, taking the Allies onto the mainland of Italy. *St David* was lost, along with many of her crew including her master, on 24 January 1944 off the beaches at Anzio on the west coast of Italy, after being bombed by the Luftwaffe.

At 5 p.m. on 26 May, the code-word 'Dynamo' was sent to the railway companies, warning them that the evacuation from Dunkirk was due to start. The operation ran from 27 May to 4 June, and the difficulty of organising it was made worse by the sudden realisation on the part of the authorities that a second evacuation was needed of many children moved from London, but who were now too close for comfort to German airfields. Neither the railways nor the military knew how many men to expect from Dunkirk; in the end, more than 338,000 were carried. This of necessity meant massive disruption to ordinary services, with even the slimmed-down wartime timetable suspended in many cases. Worst affected were services between Tonbridge and Redhill, and between Redhill, Guildford and Reading. This was an important cross-country route bypassing the London area for those troops being taken to Wales, the West Country and the Midlands. The usual passenger trains along the Tonbridge–Reading lines were suspended and replacement bus services provided, resulting in greatly extended journey times along the narrow and meandering A25.

While in many ways the whole exercise has been seen since as a masterpiece of organisation and improvisation, it took place amid chaos. No one knew how many troops would arrive, when or where, with no idea of how many were fit and how many were wounded, and still less of where to send them. Trains were turned round at Dover and sent off before the authorities had any idea of a destination, so often drivers were instructed to 'Stop at Guildford and ask where you are going to.' Volunteers tried to ensure that the arriving troops were given tea and something to eat, as well as a card so that they could write home to let their families know that they were safe. A collection at one station to provide food and drink for the troops, organised by the station master's wife, raised more than £1,000 from passengers and from people who had been drawn to the station by the continuous flood of the heavily laden troop trains. Inevitably, everything was under unforeseen pressure. One example was that at some stations used as refreshment stops, there weren't enough cups: tins had to be used as improvised cups, and just before a train left from a refreshment stop, the order was given for these to be thrown out so that the volunteers could wash them ready for the next train.

Exceptional circumstances demand exceptional measures, and the railway companies quickly agreed among themselves to provide a large pool of carriages. The GWR provided sufficient for forty trains, the LMS forty-four, the LNER forty-seven and the Southern fifty-five, a total of 186 trains of almost 2,000 carriages, with the Southern's total concealing great hardship for passengers on the non-electrified routes as the electric trains could not reach the Channel ports. Dover filled 327 trains,

Ramsgate eighty-two, and Margate seventy-five troop trains plus another twenty-five ambulance trains, while Folkestone had the surprisingly low figure of sixty-four trains. Sheerness handled seventeen trains, while there were also a small number of men landed at Newhaven and even a few at Southampton, some distance from the main evacuation scene. The busiest days were 1 June and 4 June, with as many as sixty vessels alongside at Dover at any one time on the last day. The entire operation was achieved by having holding points for empty trains at Faversham, Margate, Queenborough and Ramsgate, although at one time the system became so congested that four trains had to be held as far away as Willesden. Possibly the railways managed so well because they were used to the demand for special trains caused by major sporting events, but one general was heard to remark that he wished that the army 'could operate with as few written instructions as the Southern Railway does!'

The big bottleneck in this system was Redhill, where trains travelling from Tonbridge towards Guildford had to reverse across a completely flat junction which also had a heavy traffic of Brighton line semi-fast and stopping trains. This was not the only problem, since at one stage this station, with just three platform faces, ran short of water, not usually required for its customary service of electric trains, with only the relatively infrequent cross-country trains worked by steam at this stage. Another problem also soon surfaced, for by 4 June the station had accumulated 300 tons of ashes. Despite the awkward layout for such traffic, 80 per cent of the Dunkirk trains passed through Redhill, and most trains took no longer than four minutes to change locomotives and reverse, with the record being two and a half minutes. This was no easy task, as second locomotives had to be waiting ready for every train from the Kent coast, while others were waiting for empty trains returning to the coast. Locomotives needing coaling had to be sent as light engines to Earlswood or even Three Bridges, some 9 miles distant, as Redhill's limited facilities were soon overwhelmed and then exhausted.

THE SECOND EVACUATION

The rapid German advance westwards changed everything. At the outset, many had believed that the Second World War would see the same long drawn-out tussle on French soil that had marked the First World War. Now the authorities were embarrassed to find that some of the original areas chosen to send evacuees were no longer safe. A further evacuation was necessary, moving children from Kent (and for that matter, Essex and Suffolk as well) westwards. This started as early as 19 May 1940, using sixteen special trains to carry 8,000 children from the three most threatened counties. On 2 June, in the midst of the Dunkirk evacuation, 48,000 children were moved from towns on the east coast in seventy trains. Ten days later, on 12 June, the move of 100,000 London children to Berkshire, Somerset, the south-west and Wales started, and continued until 18 June.

As the Battle of Britain raged throughout August and into September, hop-pickers in Kent were offered the opportunity to travel westwards rather than return to London, and this required another fifteen trains for 8,000 people. In the autumn, a further evacuation was organised from London for 13,500 women and children using twenty-three trains. As the journey lengths increased and the winter weather set in, the authorities asked the railways if they could provide hot meals on the trains – a tall order since, with the exception of Pullman trains, normally only a fraction of the usual number of travellers on a train required hot meals – but this was done on condition that the escorts for the children helped with serving and washing up, and all for a shilling.

In fact, the authorities were by this time concerned that invasion was a real possibility. As the Battle of Britain turned to the Blitz, with London bombed every night bar one for sixty-seven nights, a scheme was drawn up to evacuate 746,000 people from certain parts of the south and east coasts during early summer 1941. The plans were prepared in great secrecy to avoid panic, but they called for 988 trains to be used and for the operation to be completed in just four days. Fortunately, it was not necessary.

The threat of invasion faded away and the Blitz also eased after the Germans turned their attention to the Soviet Union. Yet, even after D-day in 1944, there were other threats to contend with. The appearance of the flying bombs meant yet another evacuation. Many left on ordinary services, but the authorities sanctioned an official evacuation of children and mothers with young children, and 200,000 people were moved from London and the south coast on special trains. This was a more difficult evacuation than the earlier ones, actually carried out under attack, while the railways were busy moving reinforcements and supplies to support the fighting in France, and over a system that had already suffered five years of wartime attack and neglect.

CHANNEL ISLANDS

While Dunkirk was one consequence of the German invasion of France, the next was the realisation that the Channel Islands could not be held. For the first nine months of war, these islands had been a haven of tranquillity, although RAF and Fleet Air Arm units had been based there, and life had continued as before, including the use of the railway ships to bring the potato harvest to England. In 1940, some of the local hoteliers were even expecting holidaymakers to arrive that summer.

Realising that the Channel Islands would be almost impossible to defend and supply once France fell to the Germans, an evacuation was put in hand by the authorities. On 19 June, the British government declared the islands to be a demilitarised zone, and the RAF and Fleet Air Arm units returned home. Voluntary evacuation was offered to women and children, as well as to those men willing to volunteer to join the armed forces. Both the Great Western and the Southern Railway, which had operated a joint service before the war, with the GWR operating to the islands from Weymouth and the Southern from Southampton, put their ships at the disposal of the authorities organising the evacuation. Five Southern Railway cargo steamers were used in the evacuation, taking 8,000 people from Jersey, 17,000 from the smaller island of Guernsey and 1,500 from Alderney. These ships were hardly well suited to the purpose, although temporary shelter was provided, and the small fleet struggled to take so many people to England between 17 and 28 June. Alderney was completely evacuated, Sark almost completely, but while many on the two largest islands decided to leave, others stayed put. Then there were those who left it too late.

Despite the suspension of the Weymouth service, the two railway companies had continued operating services to the Channel Islands jointly, and their staff were asked to stay at their posts while attempts were made to continue sailings to and from the islands as far as possible, given that many ships had been taken up by the Admiralty.

Both the Southern Railway and the Great Western had agreed with the authorities that their ships would continue operating the joint services even after the evacuation ended, so that life on the Channel Islands could continue as usual. This was not necessarily a wise move, since it was inconceivable that life would not be disrupted, and certainly any shipping attempting to reach the islands would be very vulnerable. It seems incredible that the Southern Railway was expected by the government to maintain its regular services in such circumstances, even though the service was much reduced due to wartime restrictions, uncertainty and the requisition by the military of so many ships, many of which, as we have seen, had already been lost.

Nevertheless, there were twelve sailings from the islands between Sunday 23 June 1940 and Friday 28 June, when the last sailing was made during an attack on Guernsey by the Luftwaffe. Among the last passengers were thirty-eight of the forty-nine railway company staff in Guernsey, with three more definitely left behind but another eight unaccounted for at the time. On 27 June, the regular packet vessel the *Isle of Sark* had left Southampton for Jersey and Guernsey with more than 250 passengers, making the overnight passage to arrive at Jersey at 6.30 the following morning, where she was seen, but not attacked, by a German aircraft. The service also carried passengers between the islands, so that when the *Isle of Sark* reached Guernsey at 12.30 on 28 June, she had 454 passengers on board, many of whom were to continue to Southampton, although many of them took the opportunity to go ashore for the afternoon as the return trip was again to be an overnight passage. At 7 p.m., as passengers were embarking, three German aircraft attacked, bombing the pier, while the ship's AA armament went into action – an old 12-pounder and four Lewis guns. As additional aircraft attacked, more than fifty people ashore were killed and a number of small craft sunk, although the *Isle of Sark* herself was undamaged. The master was ordered to sail as soon as the tide permitted, but he held back until 10 p.m. and reached Southampton safely the following morning with 647 passengers. This was the last British ship to leave the Channel Islands.

After a German aircraft landed on Guernsey on 30 June and found that there was no resistance, German forces occupied the islands starting on 1 July. During the war, at least one message was received by *The Great Western Railway Magazine* assuring its readers that the railway company employees in Jersey were safe and well.

The Southern Railway decision, doubtless taken under government pressure, contrasts with the action of the directors of one of the main coastal and short sea shipping companies, the General Steam Navigation Company. The company had seen some of its ships taken over by the Germans and employees interned when they were caught in German ports on the outbreak of the First World War, and so it moved during the final days of peace to ensure that no ships and no employees were likely to be caught in German ports. The same measures were put in hand for those in the Low Countries once the advance westwards started. The result for both the Southern Railway and the Great Western Railway by contrast was that, when the Germans did arrive, a number of the railway employees were caught and interned. At the 1941 AGM, the chairman of the Southern Railway drew attention to this and said that special provision had been made by the company for the wives and children of these employees.

NIGHTLY EVACUEES

Trains weren't the only residents of tunnels at night. At Dover, the number of casualties during the shelling of the port and town was kept relatively low because the remaining residents spent much of their time in the caves beneath the famous white cliffs. At Chiselhurst in Kent, the caves provided a natural air-raid shelter, and many people would 'commute' by train to Chislehurst each evening to seek shelter in the caves.

While not everyone could find a cave in which to spend the night, many did move themselves and their families away from London, which meant that, despite the restricted train service, commuter traffic actually increased as many of the more affluent Londoners moved to the outer suburbs or even further out to escape the worst of the bombing.

CHAPTER 8

OPERATIONS IN WARTIME

For the passenger used to steadily improving services on the main lines, and some of the branch lines as well, the outbreak of the Second World War came as a nasty shock. Together with the blackout, cuts in railway services were among the earliest indications that life had changed for the worse. Petrol rationing affected relatively few, and food rationing was some months away. The four days that saw the Dunkirk evacuation trains run, and during which off-peak services were cut to the minimum, were bad enough, but although normal services were restored afterwards, this was not for long.

Even for those with memories of the First World War, there were many differences in wartime railway operation when comparing the two world wars. The most obvious, especially when viewed in retrospect, was the almost complete lack of amenities such as sleeping cars and restaurant cars on Second World War trains, while these facilities were reduced but never abandoned completely during the First World War. First class disappeared from London suburban journeys during the Second World War, but not during the earlier conflict, when even the Metropolitan Railway's two Pullman cars remained in service between the City of London, past Paddington and out into rural Buckinghamshire.

Perhaps more important was another difference between the two conflicts that did not appear in the timetables, but became apparent as the war dragged on. During the First World War, railway travel had been the safest mode of transport; during the Second World War, it became the most dangerous as the men, fuel and materials being moved by the railways made them prime targets. It was not necessary either for a railway line to be bombed, as an enterprising fighter pilot could be just as effective in putting a steam locomotive out of service as a bomber crew, with the difference that the former was in and out quickly, away before anti-aircraft gunners could get into their stride. It wasn't necessary to blow the wheels off a steam locomotive or put it into the middle of a large crater, as a boiler riddled with bullets, or even better, blasted apart by cannon shell, was of no use and would take some considerable time to repair, requiring highly skilled manpower and scarce raw materials, including non-ferrous metals.

Keeping the railway running was to be another problem, but one common to both wars. Men who were experienced and highly skilled could expect to be mobilised if they were reservists or called up – despite much railway work being a reserved occupation – or might already have volunteered. Locomotives and other rolling stock were also likely to be requisitioned by the military, even for use abroad. If this wasn't bad enough, the railway workshops would be forced to devote much of their capacity to war production, including even guns, tanks and landing craft, rather than keeping the railway running. The result was that increasingly the railways began to assume a battered, war-weary and unappealing appearance. Yet, traffic continued to grow, much of it military. The civilian population also made increasing demands on the railways, with many more people in work and often working well away from home, and even if everything was done to discourage unnecessary travel, understandably, people still tried to take holidays. The virtual loss of the North Sea for the movement of materials, and especially coal, meant that this traffic had to be transferred to the already overstretched railways.

Heavy use of the railways in wartime was understandable, but neglect wasn't. The Germans realised, until everything began to fall apart in 1944, that good railway maintenance was a vital part of the war effort. When they realised that the Bielefeld viaduct was a high-priority British war target, and only survived because of the difficulty of hitting it, they built a camouflaged double-track diversionary route which ran down into the valley from both sides. By the time a bomb had been developed that didn't need to hit the viaduct, but instead undermined it and brought it down, the diversionary route was well established and railway traffic was able to continue as before.

By contrast, at its most extreme, when the 15in-gauge Romney Hythe & Dymchurch Light Railway was taken over by the British Army to carry supplies to the strong defensive positions along this low-lying and vulnerable stretch of coast, it was handed back in a shocking state. Despite its narrow gauge, one of the smallest in the British Isles, during the war years it included an armoured train sporting anti-tank rifles and machine guns. Its usual rolling stock was converted to carry supplies, including many of the components and materials for the famous Pipe Line Under the Ocean (PLUTO), which was essential to keep the Normandy invasion force functioning until ports in France and the Low

Countries could be captured and cleared of mines and obstacles. Perhaps the British Army thought that they had a 'toy' railway to play with, but in fact the line had been built during the 1920s with the support of, but independently of, the Southern Railway as a means of extending passenger services across Romney Marsh.

Oddly, there was one great exception to this tale of railway disaster in the British Isles, and again this was a contrast between British and German attitudes to railways. In the Channel Islands, the railways (closed between the wars in Jersey and which had never actually existed in Guernsey, as the Guernsey Railways and Tramways Company operated buses and trams, and later just buses) were reopened and extended by the German occupation forces. In Jersey the line of the former Jersey Eastern Railway reopened between St Helier and Gorey, plus new branches into a quarry and a German fort, and the route of the former Jersey Railway was reopened not only to its old terminus at Corbière, but was also extended to Ronez Quarry some miles away in the north of the island. Indeed, for the first time both lines actually met in St Helier rather than using different termini almost a mile apart. A completely new line was laid along the coast at St Ouen's Bay.

The resurrected railway lines were laid to a variety of gauges rather than those previously used – which was understandable as the locomotives and carriages had all been either sold or scrapped – and had more in common with the lines serving the trenches on the Western Front during the First World War than with the old island railways.

These lines were exclusively for the use of the German military authorities, and islander involvement was confined to children placing stones on the tracks and inflicting a series of minor derailments that interrupted operations briefly.

REDUCTIONS AND RESTRICTIONS

Wartime meant that the railways had to economise in the provision of their services, saving fuel and making locomotive power and rolling stock available for the many specials required by the armed forces.

In addition to evacuation services and providing support for the British Expeditionary Force in France, a taste of future traffic demands arose when, in December 1939, the first Canadian troops arrived in the UK and had to be moved from the docks to their new camps and training grounds. In May 1942, there was a repeat of this performance when the first significant numbers of US personnel started to arrive, part of a steady build-up, first in anticipation of the North African landings and then, later, for the invasion of Europe. These transatlantic troop movements placed a special strain on the LMS, with Liverpool and the Clyde as the most likely points of disembarkation.

Initially, excursion and cheap day tickets were withdrawn, but day tickets were reintroduced on 9 October 1939, although with tighter conditions that meant that they were not available before 10 a.m. and could not be used on trains departing from London between 4 p.m. and 7 p.m. Monday to Friday.

After the evacuation of children was over, services returned to normal only briefly, for on 11 September, government-inspired cuts were imposed, inflicting hardship on passengers, as normal commuter traffic remained virtually at pre-war levels. Some large companies had dispersed, especially those with strategic importance such as the shipping lines, but it was not possible for everyone to do so. The usual twenty-minute suburban frequencies were cut to half-hourly, while off-peak and Sunday services became hourly. Some suburban services were cancelled completely. Not only did this lead to unacceptable levels of overcrowding with many passengers left behind, but it also meant that station dwell times were extended as passengers struggled to alight from trains or climb aboard. Journey times were extended with a national railway speed limit of 45mph. After the uproar that followed, normal services were reinstated on week days from 18 September.

Nevertheless, this was simply a temporary reinstatement and indicated that the blanket reductions of 11 September had not been properly planned. Wartime meant that services *had* to be reduced. Reductions in passenger services followed on 25 September for both the Great Western and London Midland & Scottish, with the London & North Eastern following on 2 October, and the Southern, with its extensive commuter network, on 16 October, but this time with better allowances for peak-period travel. Off-peak, most main-line services lost their hourly trains, to be replaced by a service every two hours, often on extended timings as trains called at more stations. Off-peak suburban services were hourly. On some lines services were curtailed late in the evening, but others had special late services after midnight for the benefit of shift workers. The national maximum speed limit was increased to 60mph during October.

Catering arrangements were reduced. Pullman and buffet cars were withdrawn and restaurant car service ceased on most routes. These cutbacks must have once again aroused some public reaction and been regarded as too severe, for on 1 January 1940, Pullman cars reappeared, as did pantry cars and more buffet cars.

Less obvious to the traveller, another absence from the railways during the Second World War was the travelling post office trains, withdrawn to free the lines for other more essential traffic and also release manpower for the war effort.

Some idea of the impact of the cuts and extended journey times can be gathered from a comparison between October 1938 and the same month a year later. On the Great Western, between London and Bristol, for example, the number of daily trains fell from twenty to fourteen, while the average journey time for the 118 miles increased from 135 minutes to 178 minutes, which disguises the fact that pre-war journeys included a fastest time of just 105 minutes. Its importance to the Royal Navy notwithstanding, Plymouth suffered even worse, since all trains were routed via Bristol, so that the pre-war best time of four hours five minutes and average of four hours forty-five minutes for 225 miles, stretched to 386 minutes for a journey of 246 miles, while the number of trains fell from twelve to nine daily.

Services between London and Glasgow on the London Midland & Scottish were halved from twelve trains daily to six, with the fastest time for the 401 miles stretched from six and a half hours to an average of ten hours four minutes, compared with the pre-war average of eight hours six minutes. Trains to Manchester were cut from twenty-two to fourteen daily, while the 188 miles were covered in an average of four hours fifty-two minutes compared with a 1938 average of three hours forty-three minutes and a best of three and a quarter hours. Inverness became a tedious sixteen hours twenty-six minutes from London compared with a best thirteen hours and an average fourteen and a half hours for the 568 miles pre-war, while the number of trains was halved from four to two, about the same as today if sleepers are included.

On the London & North Eastern, the Edinburgh service saw the number of trains cut from fifteen to just eight, while the journey times for the 393 miles extended from a pre-war best of six and a half hours and an average of seven hours forty-six minutes to ten hours eight minutes. The Norwich service was cut from eighteen trains daily to twelve, and the 115 miles were covered in three hours twenty-six minutes compared with a pre-war best of two hours ten minutes and an average of two hours fifty minutes.

On the Southern Railway, the service to Southampton was cut from twenty-eight to twenty trains daily and the timings for the 79 miles stretched from a pre-war best of one hour twenty-five minutes and a 1938 average of one hour fifty minutes to two hours three minutes. Portsmouth, doubtless because of the Royal Navy and the heavy commuter traffic on this line, saw its services cut slightly from forty-five to forty daily, while the journey took an average of one hour fifty-eight minutes in 1939 compared with a 1938 best of one and a half hours and an average of one hour thirty-eight minutes. Commuter traffic on its own wasn't enough to save a service, for the Brighton line suffered one of the heaviest reductions in the number of trains, more than halved from a hundred trains daily to forty-six.

There were many reasons for the extended journey times, of which the maximum speed limits were just one. Wartime shortages of materials and the disruption of the normal renewals and maintenance programme would take their toll, with many 'temporary' speed limits, while war damage became extensive, especially in the London area and along the south and east coasts. Trains had extra stops and extra carriages. Long-distance trains from some London termini would have to be divided in two to fit the platforms, with the first half pulled out of the station and then backed on to the second half to be coupled, before the journey could start. At intermediate stations, such over-long trains had to make two stops so that passengers could board and alight.

The railways were also beginning to suffer from inroads made into their rolling stock, with locomotives being requisitioned by the military and carriages converted for use on ambulance trains, some of them for the military while others were converted for the evacuation of civilian casualties in anticipation of widespread disruption by heavy bombing, although the latter were never needed.

Other measures were also necessary. Locomotives were modified, with a number fitted with condensing gear to save water and pipes for obtaining water from streams, anticipating widespread disruption to water supplies following bombing. The major stations and depots formed their own volunteer fire-fighting forces, while there were also fire-fighting trains, able to rush to wherever they might be needed, not only because of the greater speed of the railway than road transport, but also because many fires might be more easily accessible from the railway than from the road.

INCREASED GOODS TRAFFIC

The bad winter weather of January 1940 resulted in a severe shortage of coal at the power stations and factories, as well as for the railways themselves and for the ordinary householder. This was still a coal-fired society and one that is hard to conceive of today for those who are not old enough to have experienced it. The difficulties in getting coal to users were compounded by the fact that coastal shipping was regarded as impossible because of German submarine activity. Later, after the fall of Denmark and the Low Countries, it would be seen that German aerial activity was the main threat to the colliers that had plied their way down the North Sea coast from the coalfields of Fife, Northumberland, Durham and Yorkshire to ports in East Anglia and Kent, and to London itself.

In February 1940, the Mines Department asked the Railway Executive Committee to provide 'convoy coal trains' to replace the colliers and replenish stocks of coal in the south. These were trains each of fifty wagons carrying some 600 tons of coal in all. Once started these continued, so that, including an initial 140 trains to replenish the depleted stocks of coal in the south, a total of 7,757 such trains were run in 1940 alone.

Fuel supplies, especially for the Royal Air Force, were another priority. Again, with the North Sea effectively closed to British merchant shipping, the fuel trains had to be run from ports in the west to the east. This demand took up six oil trains a week fully loaded, and, once empty, four trains in the opposite direction. This cross-country operation, difficult enough in itself, had to take place by day, and the trains carrying highly flammable fuel had to avoid a 'blanket' area, a belt 30 miles deep from the coast, stretching from Plymouth to Newcastle.

After the Blitz, the railways found themselves helping in the preparations for the British response, the bombing campaign against Germany. This required the construction of a substantial number of airfields, mainly in East Anglia, while new fighter airfields were to be built in Kent and Sussex. The new airfields were deliberately sited as close as possible to railway lines, usually near small country stations with small sidings. This meant that the building materials for the airfields, including many hundreds of tons of rubble, could inflate the station's normal goods tonnage by more than ten times. The rubble had to be shipped from all over the country and naturally enough much of it came from areas that had suffered badly in the Blitz. From November 1942, six trains a day had to be routed into East Anglia, carrying on average 440 tons of rubble each, and the following year the number was stepped up to nine trains a day. In addition to the rubble trains, there were two a day with bricks and ten trains a day with other building materials, including Tarmac. As with the fuel trains, many of these trains were routed cross-country using lines not usually heavily worked.

Iron ore was no longer imported, so home sources were exploited instead. This meant a heavy demand for trains to move the iron ore from Scotland and the Midlands to the iron and steel works. While grain continued to be imported, it had traditionally entered the country by the east coast ports, but in wartime it came in from the west, so this meant additional trains, additional paths and, as we will see in Chapter 9, more goods wagons.

The need to achieve the maximum utilisation of goods wagons had been a problem recognised by the railway companies since the grouping. Among others, the Great Western had attempted to persuade its own employees and its customers to turn wagons round more quickly. In particular, the company had objected to wagons remaining unloaded for days at a time, especially once in the private sidings of major customers. It was also a problem that the railway was not advised quickly enough of wagons that were due to be collected. Under wartime pressures, the policy of encouraging a quick turn-around of wagons gained a fresh impetus. Nevertheless, it was not until 1 March 1941 that the Inter-Company Freight Rolling Stock Control was formed. Like the Railway Clearing House, this was based at Amersham. All goods wagons, whether railway or privately owned, were placed in a pool and allocated to the individual companies as required.

The Inter-Company Freight Rolling Stock Control's senior official was the chief distributor, who was advised by a Freight Rolling Stock Committee on which each of the grouped companies was represented, while the chairman was seconded from the LNER on a full-time basis to ensure his impartiality. Not only did the Inter-Company Freight Rolling Stock Control look after all of the 652,000 wagons owned by the grouped companies, and another 585,000 privately owned wagons, but it also looked after 355,000 wagon sheets, which were important because of the need to hide the nature of many wartime loads, and 212,000 ropes. Earlier, when the convoy coal trains had started, the railways were criticised by many MPs, and especially those pressing the case for nationalisation, for inefficiency in organising rolling stock. The problem was, of course, that once the privately owned wagons were taken over, they were often in the wrong place.

The usual peacetime payments made by the railway companies for using each others' wagons were suspended in wartime, but it now became essential to keep track of every wagon, with priority being given to those for coal and coke. Every station was instructed to provide a daily return of the quantity of wagons handled, broken down by the different types, and also submit its requirements for wagons, sheets and ropes for the following day. In theory, the information was received during the early evening and within twelve hours or so the allocation of wagons and, of course, sheets and ropes, would be made. In practice, it took some time for this complex system to work efficiently, but eventually it did and few consignments were delayed by more than a few hours.

All of this would have been difficult enough with computers and wagons that were bar-coded, but using manual systems a great deal of clerical work must have been necessary.

It was also essential to make the most of each wagon. Most railway wagons were 're-plated', that is they were authorised for heavier loads than in peacetime. This was the freight wagon equivalent of the overcrowded passenger train, with corridors jam-packed with standing passengers, and even standing passengers in the compartments as well. Railwaymen were assured that the new heavier loads that each wagon was deemed to be capable of were well within safety limits, but the extra weight must have contributed to the poor state of much of the track by the end of the war.

Traffic patterns changed. As the ore fields in Great Britain had to be redeveloped to replace imported ore, a pool of some 9,000 hopper wagons had to be organised early in the war, using 6,000 privately owned and 3,000 railway owned wagons, later augmented by the temporary transfer of 1,600 hopper wagons from the LNER. Hopper wagons, whatever their source, were only suitable for specialised traffic being loaded by special machinery and unloading through opening the hopper doors. This traffic was so important that the British Iron and Steel Federation ordered 1,000 new wagons and the Ministry of War Transport ordered the construction of another 2,500.

In terms of wartime 'special trains', most people think of the troop trains first, and then perhaps trains with ammunition or other war materiel. In fact, some special trains were operated on a regular basis. Many significant targets, such as the Forth Bridge carrying the line from Edinburgh and the south across the Firth of Forth to Fife and beyond, benefited from barrage balloons. London was such an important target that it had its own balloon barrage. To ensure that the balloons always had sufficient gas available, a regular service of fast, fully fitted freight trains ran nightly from Royal Air Force depots around the country to the balloon bases in the London suburbs. These were heavy trains with around forty 12-ton wagons, each of which carried a road trailer with between thirty and thirty-six cylinders of gas. Loading entailed putting a string of five wagons into a special dock so that a tractor could run straight on to the wagons and detach a trailer on each of them. The trailers were then secured firmly to the wagons, and the train marshalled. Unloading at the 'London end' of the journey used a similar technique, as did loading the 'empties'.

REDUCED FACILITIES

In addition to trimming services, as the war progressed other restrictions were applied. On 6 October 1941, under the directions of the Minister of War Transport, all London suburban trains became third class only, with the definition being that this applied to any train starting and ending its journey within the London Passenger Transport Board's area. The reasons for the move were practical, the idea being not only to make the best use of all accommodation on the reduced number of trains, but also to recognise the difficulty in finding the right class of accommodation in a hurry during the blackout. To drive the point home, carpets were removed from first-class compartments and the first-class indicators on the compartment doors painted out, while timetables and departure indicators described trains as 'Third Class Only'. After the withdrawal of first-class accommodation, blackout or not, regular travellers seemed to be able to find their way to the most comfortable part of the train and gravitated towards the superior legroom and elbow room, and plusher upholstery, of the former first-class compartments, so that these soon became shabby with intensive use.

There was constant debate over whether sleeping cars should or should not be withdrawn. Many felt that passengers needed this facility, which was once again restricted to former first-class only, but others argued that extra day carriages provided better use of the limited number of trains being run. This was predominantly a big issue for the LMS and LNER with their long Anglo-Scottish routes, but for the Great Western it was a small matter as the sleeping cars had been available on just eight daily trains pre-war, using a small fleet of just twenty-seven cars. The Southern had never offered a sleeping car service on its domestic routes, but had operated the through 'Night Ferry' service between London and Paris using train ferries, and of course this was withdrawn even before the Battle of France began. In the end, from December 1942, sleeping cars ceased to be available for civilian passengers, but a skeleton service was maintained for those travelling on government business. Even the Great Western was allowed to use ten sleeping cars to provide services from London to Plymouth, Penzance, Neyland and Newquay.

While main-line trains retained first-class accommodation, after a period of reduced catering facilities with only a limited number of trains allowed to offer them, on 22 May 1942 all catering facilities were withdrawn from trains other than a few services to the south-west on the Southern Railway, which for some reason was allowed to provide a limited service. It then became important to discourage people from unnecessary travel.

The lack of sporting events and the fact that the coastal resorts had their beaches wrapped in barbed wire, meant that normal leisure pursuits were not available. Again on the instructions of the Minister of War Transport, on 5 October 1942 off-peak cheap returns were scrapped, leaving seasons as the only 'cheap', or discounted, tickets. This gives little idea of the impact of the service on the traveller, since the 'reduced' wartime service included a substantial number of troop trains that didn't appear in the public timetable, but did take priority over almost anything else on the line, meaning that the scheduled service suffered further delays.

Throughout the war years there was an almost constant trimming of services to reduce fuel consumption. At the same time, the changing traffic patterns created by wartime saw new stations opened and some new lengths of track to meet the needs of war workers and the military. The Elham Valley line was one of a number taken over completely by the military.

In an attempt to economise, heating was another area in which fuel could be saved, so the pre-war system of switching on full heat on main-line trains between October and April when the temperature fell below 48°F at any one of a number of monitoring points, and half-heat when the temperature fell below 55°F, was reduced to having full heat when the temperature fell below 45°F and half-heat when it fell below 50°F between November and March.

Shortages of skilled staff in the workshops, and the conversion of many of these workshops to war production, as well as shortages of materials, meant that the intervals between routine overhauls were extended. Economy measures on the Great Western were typical and included a new colour scheme for passenger carriages of reddish-brown with a bronze waistline and black roof, while locomotives were painted plain green without any decorative lining out on being sent for overhaul or repair. The colour of the locomotives soon became immaterial as standards of cleanliness dropped.

Another aspect of railway operation in which standards dropped, aided by poor lighting and encouraged by wartime shortages of everything, was honesty. There was much concern about the rising level of what was described as 'pilferage' on the Great Western system, and no doubt this was matched or even exceeded on other railways.

While Britain's air-raid warning system was excellent and undoubtedly far better than anything the Germans possessed early in the war, it was always difficult to be precise about the intended target or about the number of aircraft. Inevitably, there would be areas close to a target that were included in the 'alert', and yet attracted little attention. In fact, a solitary aircraft could cause considerable inconvenience and loss of working time by prolonging an alert. There were those, of course, who became blasé about air raids – a good example of this occurred when passengers were reluctant to leave an express at York while an air raid was in progress – but railways were obviously high profile and high priority targets, so too relaxed an attitude was asking for trouble.

The real problem came with the daylight raids. Fortunately, it was soon found that many members of the ARP movement were in fact keen aircraft enthusiasts with equally keen eyesight, who could be counted on to tell whether an aircraft was friendly or not. It was found that by placing such people in positions with a good field of vision, such as on top of a high roof, a good assessment of the threat could be made, and a decision on whether to continue working or to seek shelter could follow.

RUNNING A RAILWAY IN WARTIME

None of this, of course, can give a real impression of what it must have been like operating a railway in the blackout, or of the problems experienced by individual railwaymen and women who had to report for work after a broken night's sleep in a crowded air-raid shelter, or of coming off a night shift in the morning to find that their home no longer existed, and perhaps face the loss of family members and neighbours as well. The efficient working of a railway required skill and experience, but under wartime conditions most adults had to be available for either the armed forces or prepared to be directed to essential war work. As skilled men volunteered or were conscripted into the armed forces, many of their places were taken by women. This may have been instrumental in the eventual Allied victory, as many historians believe that one factor in the defeat of Germany was that the Germans were reluctant to mobilise the civilian population and relied too heavily on slave labour and people conscripted from occupied territories or Vichy France.

Despite many railway jobs being classified as 'reserved occupations', the railways saw a growing number of their personnel leaving to join the armed forces for the duration of the war. By February 1941, no fewer than 8,401 men had left their jobs on the Great Western Railway alone, about 7.5 per cent of its total number of employees, and rather higher in terms of male employees as much office work was carried out by women. Before the war ended, the number of GWR personnel in the armed forces would almost double. In the case of the Southern Railway, some 9,000 men had been lost to the armed forces and their place was eventually taken by 8,000 women, who even undertook some of the heavier jobs, including those of porters. At first, the new recruits did not have uniforms, but this was quickly remedied. Uniforms were important on a railway not only because much of the work was dirty, but also for security and so that passengers knew who to turn to for advice and help.

Almost coinciding with the growing number of women employees was the introduction of small platform tractors to handle parcels and baggage. These improved productivity as one tractor with a driver could handle a number of trolleys, saving manpower as well as moving parcels much more quickly. On the GWR these became known as 'trolley-trains' and the major stations were the first to receive them, including Paddington, Birmingham, Cardiff, Newport and Swansea, and also Taunton and Torquay.

Despite the cut in the number of trains, passenger traffic was 3 per cent higher in December 1939 than for the previous December. As industry got into its stride and was placed on a war footing, general goods traffic rose by 51 per cent while that for coal rose by 41 per cent. Goods train mileage increased by 18 per cent. In the docks, traffic was up by 31 per cent. Employees were given the first of a series of wartime advances on their pay in recognition that the cost of living was increasing. Security considerations also meant that the regular monthly diet of statistics fed to the readers of *The Great Western Railway Magazine* had to be suspended. In the event, while this was doubtless a necessary precaution, it is now known that there were few German spies during the war, and those who did arrive were soon detected. There may have been fewer statistics, but rather more than the odd figure did leak out, especially at the Great Western's Annual General Meeting, possibly because it was felt that by the time these were announced, their intelligence value was much diminished.

The spread of rationing, introduced in early 1940, and the difficulty that many had in shopping with so many women working, and many of them working very long hours, led to a growth in the number of staff canteens on the railways. On the Great Western, rolling stock was also modified and equipped as 'mobile canteen' trains, able to be sent to wherever such facilities were needed, either because the station canteen had been bombed or because large numbers were involved in dealing with the after-effects of an 'incident'.

Air raids often caught trains in exposed positions and it was decided that to keep moving was safer than stopping. At first, the instruction was given on all railways that, on an air-raid warning being given, passenger trains were to stop and allow passengers to alight and seek shelter if they wished, after which they would continue at a maximum speed of just 15mph. As the full impact of the Blitz took effect and air raids became so frequent, this slowed traffic down to an unacceptable extent, and the instruction was revised, with trains being allowed to proceed at 25mph from early November 1940. The danger of a derailment to a train running onto bomb-damaged track at high speed during an air raid was obvious, but away from the most heavily blitzed towns, many drivers took a chance and often ignored the speed limit, guessing that the risk of bomb damage was relatively light. For freight trains, the movement under caution was just 10mph initially, later increased to 15mph.

Despite the increase in goods traffic, bogie goods wagons, among the best operated by the railways, were taken up and converted to carry anti-aircraft guns, providing twelve full trains that could be moved quickly to

Air-raid drill was a regular event in the wartime workplace. Here staff at the London Midland & Scottish temporary headquarters at the Grove, Watford, retreat to their shelter. *(IWM FLM1184)*

Women took over many jobs that were traditionally the preserve of men. This is Signalwoman Daisy Cook at Polland signal-box on the Great Western. *(IWM D17442)*

Above: Air-raid damage at Liverpool Street on the LNER. Naturally it was the London termini that were the prime targets; they were so big that they were difficult to miss. *(IWM HU58785)*

Opposite, top: Despite a 'Stay Put' campaign, many children in the initial evacuation returned home, as seen here at Euston. *(IWM HU82779)*

Opposite, bottom: Paddington also received damage from bombs, including the V-1. *(IWM HU36186)*

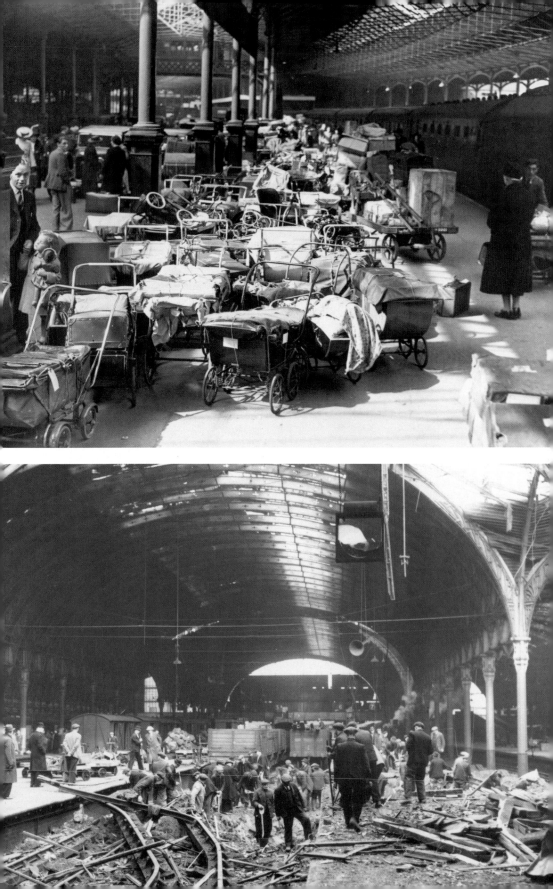

The Underground was not always safe from bombardment as bombs could, and did, penetrate Tube stations, with one of the most serious attacks at Bank station, London, on 11 January 1941. *(IWM HU66195)*

Blackout on the Underground. *(IWM HU80)*

Air-raid shelters in London included the deep-level Tube lines of London Transport – this was the scene at Elephant & Castle. *(IWM D1569)*

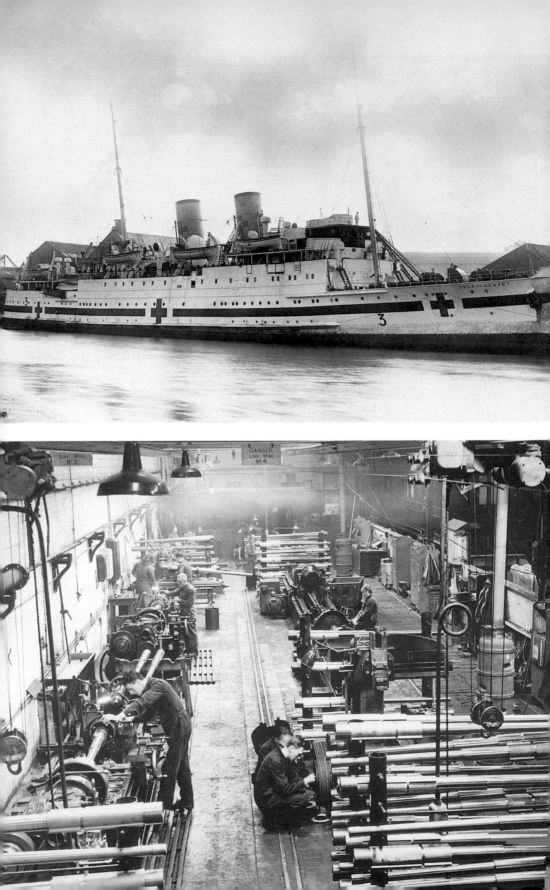

Above: Wartime precautions included special gas masks that enabled the wearer to continue working, as with these young women on the London & North Eastern Railway switchboard. *(IWM KY3159D)*

Opposite, top: While railwaymen were called up and locomotives requisitioned, an early demand was for the railway ferries – this was the Southern Railway steamer SS *Isle of Jersey* on war service as a hospital ship. *(NRM 366/69)*

Opposite, bottom: The railway workshops were more preoccupied with production for the war effort than giving care and attention to locomotives and carriages – here producing guns at Eastleigh Works on the Southern Railway.

Railway personnel hit back in the only way that they could, by contributing to company 'Spitfire Funds'. This is a Spitfire MkV of No. 222 Squadron at North Weald, named *Flying Scotsman* because it was paid for by LNER personnel. *(IWM TR21)*

Later in the war, attacks by flying bombs brought about a further evacuation, shown here as schoolchildren wait for a train at Surbiton on 11 July 1944. *(NRM 1155/36/63)*

any location needing additional AA defences. Three of the trains were manned by members of the Free Polish Army.

Shortages of skilled staff in the workshops and the conversion of many workshops to war production, as well as shortages of materials, meant that the intervals between routine overhauls were extended. The railway companies were also severely restricted in the type of steam locomotives they could build, but new building was allowed, both to replace loco-motives lost to enemy action and also to ensure that sufficient power was available for the many military specials. In theory, just two standard types were allowed. However, before this happened, on the Southern Railway, where there was a dire shortage of large locomotives, the wily chief mechanical engineer, Oliver Bulleid, introduced his famous 'air-smoothed', as opposed to 'streamlined', Pacifics, or so-called 'spam cans' because of their shape, by convincing the authorities that these were really mixed-traffic locomotives. He compensated by also introducing a utility 0–6–0 design of unsurpassed ugliness that lacked anything that could be eliminated, to save on scarce materials. Railwaymen had to be flexible, as they sometimes found themselves with unfamiliar equipment. In 1943, the 'British Railways' were presented with additional locomotive power from across the Atlantic with the loan of 2–8–0 American locomotives.

EMPLOYEE COMMUNICATIONS

The railway companies continued to provide news and information for their employees despite wartime restrictions on the dissemination of information for security reasons, and the need to conserve paper. The Southern Railway cut its employee magazine back to six issues a year instead of appearing monthly. *The Great Western Railway Magazine* continued to appear monthly, but its size was reduced so that at one time it consisted of just sixteen pages on very poor-quality paper. Unlike the Great Western and the Southern, the LMS abandoned its house publications at the outset of war, although admittedly there were three of these, *LMS Magazine*, *On Time* and *Quota News*, and these were replaced by a monthly newsletter, *Carry On*, which was provided free. Lord Stamp provided a message in the first issue with the headline 'Railways Vital to Nation's Cause: Whatever Befalls, We Must Carry On':

It will ever be a source of pride to those connected with the railways that when war did come it found us prepared to the last man and the last vehicle to play our part speedily, safely, and efficiently in the sudden special movements of traffic. . . . May we be able to say – as was said of the railways twenty years ago – that when the final victory is won, our share in it shall have been a worthy one.

Nevertheless, communications with employees in wartime were also taken over to some extent by the state. The magazines or newsletters provided for employees were subjected to censorship, and firm rules were laid down that editors had to follow. Over and above that, the Ministry of Information published hard-hitting posters that were intended to dispel rumours or careless talk. Railway workers were prime targets, as the very nature of their work meant that they knew much about the war effort. Troop trains were an obvious example, but they also knew if trains were moving munitions or even large aircraft parts, a new wartime traffic for the Great Western among others, or armoured vehicles.

Typical of these was a poster intended for railway premises:

If you've news of our munitions
KEEP IT DARK
Ships or 'planes or troop positions
KEEP IT DARK
Lives are lost through conversation
Here's a tip for the duration
When you've got private information
KEEP IT DARK

Another poster was more direct:

YOU
Know more than other people.
You are in a position of trust.
Don't let the fighting forces down.
A few careless words may give something away
that will help the enemy and cost us lives.
Above all, be careful what you say to strangers
and in public.

Communities and businesses started collections and events to raise funds to buy aircraft for the RAF, and the railway companies also ran 'Spitfire Funds'. In the case of the Southern Railway, a small plaque next to the cockpit proclaimed the company's involvement and the aircraft was named *Southern Spitfire*. The directors of the Great Western contributed the first £500 of the £5,000 target for their Spitfire. The LNER Spitfire was named *Flying Scotsman* in honour both of the express locomotive and the famous London to Edinburgh express.

Alone of the railway companies, the LNER decided to establish its own medal for heroism in wartime, and it was soon to prove to be justified.

CHAPTER 9

EXPANDING THE RAILWAY

Despite the shortages of manpower and materials and the fact that the state was a careless user of the assets of the railways, some new lines and new equipment did prove necessary over and above the repairs to war-damaged infrastructure. Investment during the war years was kept to the minimum because of the shortages, plus the fact that the country had been effectively bankrupted by the war, almost before the fighting started.

The way in which Britain's railways developed piecemeal had meant that there were some good cross-country connections, as railways had been developed to connect Edinburgh and Glasgow, Manchester and Liverpool, and the towns in Lancashire and Yorkshire. Even so, the railways had as their centre of operations London, the capital, where all of the 'Big Four' main-line companies had their main termini. Unfortunately, because the initial movement of troops was from all parts of the United Kingdom to the Channel ports, it became essential to bypass London, otherwise unacceptable congestion would have arisen. This situation was soon repeated in reverse with the evacuation from Dunkirk, and then repeated again with the Normandy landings and the need to sustain a growing number of troops in Europe.

The railway system then had to handle troops coming from across the Atlantic and needing to be moved to bases all over the country, but mainly in the south, while for reasons to do with the ebb and flow of war, it was often not known until the last minute whether the arrival point would be on the Clyde or the Mersey.

In among these mass movements of men and their equipment, there was the need to repel an expected invasion somewhere along the south coast of England.

London proved to be a major obstacle to most of these movements. It was not so much a case that there were no lines around or through London, but that the capacity of these was limited. These lines had been built when railway travel was in its infancy and traffic flows were small, while the size of railway vehicles was also limited. There had been a plan for a line from Charing Cross to Euston, but this had not gone ahead, and the arrival of the 'Hampstead Tube', which later developed into the Northern Line, had seemed to take care of most of the traffic. Yet twentieth-century wartime traffic flows were far heavier and more urgent than those of nineteenth-century peacetime.

ACROSS LONDON

There were four routes for railway traffic crossing London from north to south. These were:

1. The North & South West Junction line from Willesden, on the London Midland & Scottish, and South Acton to Kew Bridge on the Southern Railway, where there was a triangle junction with the line from Barnes to Feltham via Gunnersbury and Richmond.
2. The West London Extension, again from the LMS at Willesden, and the Great Western at Old Oak, to both the Western and Eastern sections of the Southern Railway at Clapham Junction and Battersea respectively.
3. The City Widened Lines of the Metropolitan Railway that ran from the Great Western, the LMS and the London & North Eastern to Ludgate Hill, Blackfriars Bridge and on to Herne Hill.
4. The East London Line, originally the East London Railway, which was the only one to pass under the Thames in a tunnel, and at the time was part of the London Passenger Transport Board's Metropolitan Line. This linked the LNER, formerly the Great Eastern, at Stratford with the Southern Railway at New Cross.

Of these, options 3 and 4 were regarded as vulnerable, and indeed, at the height of the Blitz seemed to be so, especially when the line to Herne Hill was disrupted by the bombing of Southwark Bridge. To avoid disruption, a new connection was built running from the LNER at Harringay to Gospel Oak on the LMS. From there it ran on to the Great Western at Acton and then to the Southern Railway by way of Kew Bridge or the West London Extension. The work was regarded as being sufficiently important that it was completed during 1940, just in time for the heavy air raids.

In peacetime, much of the traffic from the Midlands and the north had been routed via Banbury, which handled traffic both from the LNER coming south from Manchester and Sheffield, and from the GWR.

Nevertheless, Banbury was not well equipped to handle a massive growth in traffic, especially if lines across London were disrupted, and Reading was little better, with the line from Banbury having to cross the busy Great Western main line to reach the Southern Railway.

The solution was to build what amounted to a railway bypass of London. Of necessity this was some distance from the capital, both to avoid disruption from heavy air raids and also to utilise existing lines as far as possible. The start of this massive loop was the old London & North Western line from Cambridge to Oxford, which crossed the LNER from King's Cross at Sandy, the LMS lines from St Pancras at Bedford, the LMS lines from Euston at Bletchley, the LNER lines from Marylebone at Calvert, and the Great Western route from Paddington to Birmingham at Bicester. There were good existing connections in and out of this line at Bedford and Bletchley, but at Sandy and at Oxford time-consuming shunting movements would be necessary, so here again new connections were hastily installed and opened during 1940. There was no link at all at Calvert, so a completely new link was created.

INCREASING CAPACITY

The growth in demand and the completely new traffic flows created by wartime meant that many of the single- and double-tracked lines were inadequate. In some cases quadrupling took place, while in other cases additional passing loops were built on single-track lines and long-running loops on double-tracked lines, and what might be described as holding yards where several slow-moving goods trains could be kept out of the way of other faster traffic.

These works sound simple in themselves, but of course this was often not the case. One GWR/LMS venture, for example, required seven underbridges to be reconstructed, apart from work on retaining walls for embankments and land drainage.

Further north, with so many transatlantic convoys starting or finishing in Scotland, the west-coast line needed increased capacity. Just north of Carlisle, the line was indeed quadrupled, but after a junction with the LNER, it came down to double track, including the vulnerable crossing of the River Eden. The solution was to build an additional double-track bridge over the river, and extend the goods lines in the area. This required a new viaduct with seven main spans each of 46ft and two approach spans of 35ft.

On the other side of the country, the east coast main line also needed attention, especially as this was the route taken by so many of the coal trains carrying traffic displaced from the coasting trade. While the double-tracked line between York and Northallerton had been improved during the 1930s with some stretches of quadruple and triple tracks, and the installation of colour light signalling, a number of bottlenecks remained, including those at Skelton Bridge, Raskelf, Sessay and Thirsk. York was also a bottleneck itself, especially since a major resignalling programme had been abandoned in 1940 because of the other demands of wartime. It was also the case that the York resignalling would have put a lot of authority in a single, vulnerable, control centre. Nevertheless, without the resignalling, York also featured massive sidings on both sides of the line to accommodate goods trains waiting for a route. Again, main-line widening was carried out, initially quadrupling the line between Pilmoor and Thirsk, while there were also further lines built, although in some cases in only one direction.

MOTIVE POWER

The austerity measures put in place on the outbreak of war meant that the railways were restricted to building mixed-traffic 4–6–0 locomotives and heavy freight 2–8–0 locomotives. The programme was not solely concerned with the wartime needs of the railways, but also those of the British Army that might need substantial numbers of locomotives at short notice for service overseas. As mentioned elsewhere, in December 1941 the Ministry of War Transport decreed that a standard locomotive based on the LMS Stanier 2–8–0 was to be the only locomotive that could be built in the railway workshops, although it then relented and allowed limited production of the general traffic 4–6–0 'Hall' class locomotives of the Great Western. The LMS built thirty of the 2–8–0s at Crewe and another seventy-five at Horwich, but many more were built by the other companies. The GWR built eighty at Swindon, the LNER built fifty-three at Darlington and fifty at Doncaster, while the Southern built fourteen at Ashford, ninety-three at Brighton and twenty-three at Eastleigh. Nevertheless, these were far from the only steam locomotives built in wartime.

The LNER's obsession with speed and its prestige expresses had meant that it was short of the mixed-traffic and heavy freight locomotives that were to be so necessary in wartime. This situation was made worse by the requisitioning of many of its useful 2–8–0 ex-Great Central locomotives by the War Office. The V2 series of 2–6–2 locomotives had been very successful and useful, but their axle loadings confined them to the main lines. There were many elderly 4–4–0s, 4–4–2s and 4–6–0s that also needed to be replaced, especially since they dated from the pre-grouping companies, and some standardisation would be an advantage. The answer was the V4 2–6–2, an attractive and sophisticated engine that embodied all of Sir Nigel Gresley's experience. Two prototype locomotives were built, but these were not the simple, rugged locomotives that wartime austerity required. They were not wasted, but they became yet another of the many classes of goods locomotives infesting the LNER. Some LNER men believed that, had it not been for Gresley's sudden death, the V4 could have become the standard locomotive, as subsequent experience proved it to be reliable and efficient. This was to misunderstand the thinking of those with responsibility for procurement in wartime, when proven reliability was needed rather than new and untested designs, no matter how brilliant.

Gresley's protégé, Oliver Bulleid, had taken over as chief mechanical engineer at the Southern Railway in 1937, and inherited a railway in which development of larger and more powerful locomotives of the kind favoured by the LNER had been neglected, partly owing to the demands of electrification, but also because of weight restrictions on many lines. He pressed successfully for the introduction of powerful 4–6–2 locomotives, despite severe wartime restrictions on the type and size of locomotives that could be built. Against the visual evidence, Bulleid claimed that his new designs were for general-purpose duties, and succeeded in building no fewer than 140 Pacific locomotives of the 'Merchant Navy', 'West Country' and 'Battle of Britain' classes, introducing many new features such as completely enclosed chain-driven valve gear and welded fireboxes, and an improved working environment for the enginemen. At the other end of the scale, he produced a true austerity 0–6–0 freight locomotive, the Q1 class, of outstanding ugliness, but with 30 per cent more tractive effort than the original Q class, and only a slight increase in axle loading. The Bulleid Pacifics incorporated many features that were to be introduced into post-nationalisation designs, and they were also more economical in their use of coal than the 'Britannia' class which they closely resembled, but also had their weaknesses, including poor forward visibility, and were prone to often catastrophic mechanical failures.

In his design, Bulleid went against the trend for larger coupled wheels for high-stepping express locomotives and chose a wheel diameter of 6ft 2in. It was this that allowed him to argue that these were general-purpose locomotives, which was important as express passenger locomotive construction had been banned. The first of the class appeared during the dark days of 1941, marking a break with all previous designs and using an 'air-smoothed' exterior design rather than the streamlining that had been so popular with the LNER and LMS immediately before the war. The new locomotives were a massive step up in power, with a 47 per cent increase on the grate area compared with the 'Lord Nelson' class, and a 38 per cent increase in heating surface, allied to the highest boiler pressure so far on any production express locomotive, giving a nominal tractive power of 37,500lb. The reason for so much innovation was the need to observe weight restrictions on many Southern routes, allied to a shortage of space within the resultant design. The limited publicity opportunities allowed in wartime, when even a new locomotive was a contribution to the effort, showed these locomotives at the head of goods trains, no doubt to appease the politicians and bureaucrats.

Despite austerity, the 'Merchant Navy' class introduced new standards of driver comfort and gave the Southern a massive step-change in locomotive power, but mechanically required considerable attention. Nevertheless, Bulleid persisted with the novel features and retained them when he introduced his lighter-weight 'West Country' and 'Battle of Britain' classes starting in 1945.

Wartime meant that the predominantly passenger-based Southern Railway was carrying much increased volumes of freight. Rather than build more of the 0–6–0 freight locomotives, towards the end of the war Bulleid modified the design in an attempt to produce more power from a locomotive of the same weight, again with increased boiler pressure in his new class Q1. A true utility look was conveyed by the simplest possible boiler casing and the absence of running plate and splashers. In a word, the Q1 was ugly, and compared unfavourably in appearance with the relatively handsome Stanier 2–8–0 standard wartime locomotive.

Unlike the Great Western's 'Hall' class, which were allowed to be built in limited numbers by the Ministry of War Transport, building of the 'Merchant Navy' class was interrupted by the austerity locomotive ruling of late 1941.

New construction was only part of the story though, as many loco-motives were substantially upgraded during major overhauls, especially when their boilers wore out. Some existing locomotives when returned to service, especially on the LMS, had little of the original about them other than the frames. These were extreme examples, but on the Great Western, on overhaul many locomotives received much improved levels of superheating.

Although not actually intended for the 'Big Four' companies, the North British Locomotive Company produced its WD 2–8–0 design for use by the British Army abroad. Many of these were run on Britain's railways before the invasion of Normandy, doubtless to iron out any problems before sending them abroad, as well as helping the railway companies through their own locomotive shortages. The LNER had most of these (350), doubtless to compensate for the loss of so many of its own locomotives, while the LMS and the Southern had fifty apiece. Post-war, many of these were brought home and put to work on the railways, where some regarded them as the best heavy freight locomotive available.

The S.160 class American locomotives, also 2–8–0, arrived in 1943 and, after modification by the Great Western, were put into service on a 'pooled' basis, at the end of the year, the Great Western having 174, followed by the LNER with 168, the LMS with 50 and the Southern with 6.

PASSENGER ROLLING STOCK

Wartime construction of new passenger rolling stock virtually ceased due to the austerity drive. Nevertheless, the Great Western was allowed to complete the final stage of its railcar programme, largely because work was too far advanced and much of the equipment, such as the engines, had already been built. In any case, diesel railcars required a third less manpower in operation, and much less in maintenance, than did steam trains, even as steam railmotors. The Southern Railway was also allowed to build two units of a new class of suburban electric multiple unit, on which the design work had been started before the war, but these were to a new severe utility specification, although not quite as bad as some of the wartime utility-bodied buses which had wooden seats.

While services were cut back in wartime, the Southern Railway had been suffering capacity problems even before the outbreak of war on its suburban services. To alleviate overcrowding, the first step was to convert a large number of three-car units to four cars by using trailer carriages from electric multiple units mothballed as a result of the wartime reductions in frequencies.

Limited construction of a new class of suburban electric rolling stock was permitted. Initially undesignated, but later becoming known as 4 SUB, these were of all-metal construction using welded and curved body sides to increase capacity. The first appeared early in 1941, with two motor coaches having a motorman's compartment, a guard's compartment and nine third-class compartments each with seats for twelve passengers, a trailer with two third, six first and two third-class compartments, with the first-class compartments each having ten seats, and another trailer with eleven third-class compartments. Overall accommodation was for sixty first-class and 396 third-class passengers. Later that year, by which time all London suburban services had become third class only by official decree, a second set appeared with third-class seating throughout, giving a total of 468 seats, indicating that the numbers of compartments and their dimensions were the same as on the original, so that conversion back to first- and third-class accommodation was envisaged after the war. This was all that was allowed for the time being, but a further seven sets were built to this specification between January and April 1945, by which time new construction was becoming acceptable again.

GOODS ROLLING STOCK

The 're-plating' of goods wagons to allow them to be more heavily loaded has already been mentioned. This was when the parsimony of the colliery owners in not organising their sidings for efficiency and adopting new higher capacity wagons began to tell. The country was being expected to fight a modern war, which also meant an industrial war, using wagons better suited to the Victorian railway.

The importance of keeping industry and the armed forces supplied meant there was not the same reluctance to build new goods wagons as there was for passenger stock. In effect, coal and petrol were more important than passengers. As the motor vehicle had become more commonplace, oil wagons had become an increasingly common sight on the pre-war railway. At the outbreak of the Second World War, companies already had many six-wheeled oil wagons, and their oil-carrying capacity was boosted during the war by the arrival of eight-wheeled bogie oil wagons from the United States. These carried 40 tons of oil. The barrels and the bogies were shipped as dismantled units and assembled by the Great Western Railway after arrival in the UK.

Other new wagons included those necessary for new wartime traffic, such as tanks, while other freight rolling stock was converted for new uses. Additional grain wagons were required with the east-coast ports no longer available to receive shipments, and the railway companies' own stock of just 300 bulk-grain wagons was inadequate for the task. This was solved by converting LNER 20-ton hopper coal wagons, of which almost 250 were needed for this traffic. Insulated banana vans were no longer needed for bananas, as these weren't imported during the war years, and instead were converted to help with the transport of fresh meat.

The pre-war railways had in fact been capable of carrying single items as big as 120 tons on special low-loader bogie wagons, but tanks required a level platform, even though they were only a fraction of this weight. Covered vans already existed to carry motor cars from the factories to distribution centres or the docks, and these provided the basis for some wartime conversions.

The problems of wartime iron-ore traffic have already been mentioned, as has the need for more wagons, with the British Iron and Steel Federation ordering another 1,000 22-ton steel hopper wagons, while the Ministry of War Transport authorised the construction of another 2,500 wagons to the LNER design.

EXTRA-SPECIAL TRAINS

The wartime railway ran many special trains, from troop trains to evacuee trains to different kinds of freight train. Some peacetime special trains also remained, of which the most obvious was the Royal Train. Indeed, this had to have its pre-war London & North Western livery of brown and white changed to make it seem less special as King George VI and Queen Elizabeth made many journeys, usually to visit communities that had suffered in the Blitz. This was in complete contrast to the leaders of the 'other' side, who did no such thing.

Nevertheless, there were at least four other 'special' trains as the war progressed, including one for the Prime Minister, Sir Winston Churchill, and another for the Chief of the Imperial General Staff, General Sir Alan Brooke, later Field Marshal Lord Alanbrooke. Churchill awarded Sir Alan a special train rather as if he were bestowing a present. The other two ran on Britain's railways for a while, then after the invasion of Normandy, followed their VIPs to Europe. These were the special trains for the Supreme Commander, Allied Forces Europe, the American General

Eisenhower, whose train was code-named 'Alive', and for his deputy, the British General Sir Bernard Montgomery, later Field Marshal Lord Montgomery of Alamein, whose train was code-named 'Rapier'.

'Alive' was assembled and converted by the Great Western at Swindon and consisted of:

Two covered carriages for baggage and staff cars
Utility van for boiler and generator for when the train was without a locomotive
Two corridor brake thirds for staff and stores
Corridor third for staff
Restaurant car
Conference saloon
Two sleeping cars: ex-LNER first-class sleeper with four berths converted to form saloon; sleeper converted from corridor third to provide 32 berths
Six covered trucks for baggage and cars

'Rapier' was prepared by the LNER at Doncaster and used mainly ex-LNER rolling stock, consisting of:

Two first brakes
First saloon
Third restaurant car incorporating office
First sleeper, with a bath fitted
Two LMS covered carriage trucks for cars and stores
Charging van

CHAPTER 10

IN THE FRONT LINE

There were several aspects to the history of the Southern Railway during the Second World War. As with the other companies, there was the heavy damage inflicted on the system, its rolling stock and personnel by the war, with heavy bombing for a full year from mid-1940, until the demands of Operation Barbarossa, the German invasion of the Soviet Union, provided some relief. After this hiatus there were still periods of bombing, including a 'mini-blitz' and the so-called 'Baedeker Raids', before the advent of the V-1 and V-2 missiles or flying bombs. In fact, the Southern suffered the highest level of damage per route mile of any of the 'Big Four' companies.

In addition, there were the demands placed on the system which handled the dispatch of the British Expeditionary Force to France and joined the other companies and London Transport in the dispersal of schoolchildren away from the major cities. It was the Southern, with lines serving a string of ports along the English Channel, that bore the brunt of the dispatch of the BEF to France, the return of the BEF and other troops from France, and then supported the British and American forces in France after the Normandy invasion. The Southern's fleet of ferries played an important role in the evacuation of Dunkirk and the Channel Islands, and ships were lost.

The Southern Railway had been the most active in extending new forms of propulsion over its metals, with the world's largest electrified system on the outbreak of war. The entire inner and outer suburban system was electrified, as well as the main lines to Portsmouth, Littlehampton, Bognor Regis, Brighton and Eastbourne, and even some secondary routes such as those to Aldershot and Alton, and Maidstone. As war threatened, the Southern's directors and senior management were concerned over whether or not the electrified lines would cope with the heavy punishment of a bombing campaign. As the blitz developed, it was discovered that the main factor was whether any trains could run at all. Electric trains could run wherever steam trains could, with the added advantage of not needing turntables or coaling and watering facilities. They also had the advantage, as we have already seen, of not leaving large quantities of ash to be removed. As with the other railways, in the four years between Dunkirk and the Normandy landings, the Southern was under intense pressure supplying industry and the armed forces; providing many troop trains, often at extremely short notice; suffering a shortage of personnel as many volunteered to join the armed forces; and coping with a shortage of spares and equipment for maintenance as so much had to be diverted to the war effort. It was hardest for the Southern Railway, however, as it not only had major naval and army bases within its area, but was also the railway closest to France and Belgium and therefore German airfields in these occupied territories. Again, as with the other companies, many of the Southern's ferries and packets were also 'taken up from trade', and pressed into the war effort.

The presence of the armed forces in its area was not a small one, even in peacetime. There were naval bases at Portsmouth, Chatham, Gosport and Portland, while the demands of Plymouth were shared with the Great Western. The army was at Aldershot and on Salisbury Plain, where it had extensive training grounds. The Royal Air Force had many of its fighter stations strung along the south of England, especially in Kent and Sussex.

ONTO A WAR FOOTING

Naturally, the Southern matched the other companies in its efforts to move from peacetime to wartime, giving priority to placing air-raid notices in the compartments of trains on the Eastern Section, which was judged most likely to be affected because of its proximity to Europe, and at Victoria the station lights were replaced by blue lights. Blackout was enforced from 2 September, and the next day Britain and France were at war with Germany.

The demands of the country at war meant that the Southern's general manager, Gilbert Szlumper, who had taken over from Sir Herbert Walker on his retirement in 1937, was soon transferred to the War Office as Director-General of Transportation, a testament to his abilities, and his place as general manager at Waterloo was taken by Eustace Missenden, who had been traffic manager, with John Elliot, a former journalist who had handled the Southern's publicity as his deputy.

Alone among the main-line railway companies, the Southern was overwhelmingly a passenger railway. It did carry freight, but the main traffic was coal, both for the coal merchants who often traded from its station yards and for its own dwindling fleet of steam locomotives. The impact of the cuts on passenger services imposed shortly after the outbreak of war hit the Southern harder than most, for although its autumn day-tripper market had all but disappeared, it still had to serve its massive commuter market. These were people who had been lured to the dormitory towns and villages served by the 'Southern Electric' by advertisements with headlines such as 'Live in Kent and be content' or 'Live in Surrey far from worry'. The usual twenty-minute suburban frequencies were cut to half-hourly, while off-peak and Sunday services became hourly. A number of services were cancelled completely, including London Bridge–Streatham Hill and Holborn Viaduct–Herne Hill–Orpington. After the reductions were reversed on weekday services, a new timetable followed on 16 October, still with more reductions than in peacetime, but with better allowances for peak-period travel.

Cannon Street was closed between 10 a.m. and 4 p.m. Monday to Friday and after 7.30 p.m. on weekdays, as well as closing all day on Sunday. Services were suspended between Holborn Viaduct and Dartford via Nunhead, and between London Bridge and Streatham Hill and Victoria to Beckenham Junction, with only a peak-period service Waterloo–Putney–Wimbledon and to Addiscombe. On the Eastern and Central sections a number of stations lost their off-peak direct services. On the busy Brighton line, the only non-stop trains were in the rush hours, and their journey times were extended by the implement-ation of the maximum speed limits. Off-peak, there were just three trains an hour on the Brighton line, worse than half the pre-war service, as through services to Worthing and Littlehampton were only available at peak periods. Waterloo to Reading, never a fast line compared with the Great Western run from Paddington, became an even more tedious stopping service after a call at Richmond, and the Alton line lost its rush-hour extras.

These cuts were accompanied by reductions in catering arrange-ments, with Pullman and most buffet cars being withdrawn and restaurant-car services ceasing on the Portsmouth Direct. Once again, off-peak suburban services were hourly, although the busy line from Charing Cross to Bexleyheath and Sidcup remained half-hourly. On some lines, such as the South London, services were curtailed late in the evening, but others had special late services running after midnight for the benefit of shift workers.

These cutbacks must have aroused some public reaction and been regarded as too severe, for on 1 January 1940, Pullman cars reappeared, as did pantry cars, and there was an increase in the number of buffet cars, while restaurant service resumed on the Portsmouth Direct. A number of services were also reinstated during peak hours, as were some of the cancelled rush-hour extra trains.

Despite these concessions, made while the 'Phoney War' persisted, after the fall of France many fresh restrictions were imposed. Throughout the war years there was an almost constant trimming of services to reduce fuel consumption and eliminate under-used train miles. Shoreham Airport Halt closed on 15 July 1940, while on 6 January 1941, Crystal Palace (High Level) lost its direct services and was worked by a shuttle from Nunhead, before being closed completely on 1 May 1944. Waterloo–East Putney–Wimbledon ended altogether on 5 May. On 1 January 1942, Bishopstone Beach Halt was closed. While main-line trains retained first-class accommodation, on 22 May 1942 they lost all catering facilities on the electrified lines, although some service was maintained on the steam-hauled trains to Devon and Cornwall, because of the longer distances involved. The Pullman cars were all taken out of the Brighton line sets and stored, as were the buffet cars on the 4 BUF main-line electric sets. Restaurant and pantry cars remained in the sets because of their higher seating capacity, but with the catering areas locked out of use. Later that same year, many suburban electric multiple units were lengthened from three to four carriages by the simple expedient of breaking up the trailer sets, many of which were by this time stored due to the reduced services on offer, and inserting an additional trailer in the motor sets. This eliminated some shunting and the time and manpower needed to insert extra sets at peak periods, and also provided extra accommodation when a single set was being operated.

The bad weather of late December 1939 to the end of January 1940 has already been mentioned. Accustomed to the Southern's normal quiet efficiency, passengers suffered the worst disruption many had seen.

The railway contribution to the Dunkirk evacuation and the efforts made by the GWR and the SR in the Channel Islands have also been covered. What made the Southern different was that, after the fall of France and the Low Countries, the authorities found that some of the original areas chosen for evacuees were no longer safe and a further evacuation was necessary, moving children from Kent westwards. This started as early as 19 May 1940, using sixteen special trains to carry 8,000 children from the three most threatened counties. On 2 June, in the midst of the Dunkirk evacuation, 48,000 children were moved from towns on the east coast in seventy trains. Ten days later, on 12 June, the move of 100,000 London children to Berkshire, Somerset, the south-west and Wales started, and continued until 18 June. The Southern's share of this exodus was 42,391 children in eighty-four trains from Waterloo, Vauxhall, Clapham Junction and a number of suburban stations.

As with the original evacuation, many parents changed their minds at the last minute and kept their children, so that a train from Vauxhall to north Cornwall intended for 600 passengers only carried 417 children and 32 adults.

Elsewhere, civilians found themselves not simply facing the possibility of invasion and the likelihood of German bombing, but German shellfire as well. The population of Dover fell from around 40,000 pre-war to around 23,000 after Dunkirk. Of course, some of these may have moved not because the town was vulnerable, but because the curtailment of the cross-Channel ferries would have meant that many jobs were no longer available and the labour would have been directed elsewhere, while the crews of the Channel packets would have often followed their ships as they were diverted to war work. Nevertheless, the shelling of Dover was relentless. Between three and four thousand shells landed on Dover and the surrounding area between 1940 and 1944, with another 1,800 falling into the harbour or offshore, as against 464 bombs, three parachute mines and three flying bombs. During the final days of the heavy shelling, on 13 September 1944, a shell scored a direct hit on the Priory station – the station for the town as opposed to ferry travellers – and several people were killed and many more injured.

During summer 1944, the appearance of the flying bombs meant yet another evacuation, although at first this was unofficial. Once again the authorities sanctioned an official evacuation of children and mothers with young children, and 200,000 people were moved from London and the south coast on special trains, and many more left on ordinary services. This was a more difficult evacuation than the earlier ones, largely because previous evacuations had been carried out in anticipation of attack, but the latest evacuation was carried out under attack. It was also carried out while the Southern especially was busy moving reinforcements and supplies to support the fighting in France, and, of course, it was using a system that had suffered five years of wartime attack and neglect.

Nevertheless, it was not always a question of reduced services and station closures. Changing traffic patterns created by wartime saw a new halt opened at Hilsea, close to Portsmouth Airport, to meet the needs of war workers. On 11 October 1942, a new spur was opened at Crayford from the Sidcup loop to the North Kent line. Another halt was opened at Longcross, between Virginia Water and Sunningdale, on 3 May 1943, and one was also opened at Upper Halliford, near Shepperton, on 1 May 1944.

The next step was to discourage unnecessary travel. On the instructions of the Minister of War Transport, on 5 October 1942 off-peak cheap returns were scrapped, leaving seasons as the only 'cheap', or discounted, tickets. Evidence of the impact of the economy measures came at a conference on fuel in 1944, which showed that in each of the last two years before the war, the Southern had operated 220 million car miles and used 530 million units of electricity, while its reduced wartime service was using 164 million car miles and 409 million units. The wartime service also seemed to use slightly more power per car mile than the peacetime service, despite the speed restriction, possibly due to extra stops. In an attempt to economise on electricity, coasting marks were sited for stopping trains, and while there were no such marks for non-stop trains, an unofficial system of 'on' and 'off' points was established. Heating was another area in which fuel was saved.

However, the pressure on the Southern Railway was such that not all production and innovation could be abandoned. To get the most out of the electrified lines, the first of two electric locomotives, mothballed on the outbreak of war, was completed and ready for trials in 1941, and a second was completed in 1943. The railway also received the first of the 0–6–0 Q1-class of tender utility locomotives and a token number of US-built tank engines after these had been modified to run on British lines. Earlier, wartime restrictions were not enough to stop Oliver Bulleid building the first of his magnificent 'Merchant Navy' class and the smaller 'West Country' and 'Battle of Britain' classes. The only oddity was that the 'Merchant Navy' class locomotives were too heavy to take boat trains into the docks at Southampton, but post-war they were to excel on cross-Channel boat trains and, not surprisingly, the first was named *Channel Packet.*

HELPING THE WAR EFFORT

The Southern played an important part in the concentration of personnel, equipment and supplies in preparation for the D-day landings in Normandy. The landings also affected the Southern's traffic in another way as, added to the normal wartime restrictions, from 2 April 1944 visitors were banned from the south coast because of the military preparations, and a number of main-line services were suspended. These restrictions were eased after the landings.

Southampton Docks played a major role during the preparations for D-day, with many of the landing ships loaded there, while the Western Section was heavily used by goods trains moving equipment and supplies to the docks. One small branch-line station, Dunbridge, near Romsey, gives a good indication of the impact of the run-up to D-day. In June 1938 this small station had handled just 182 goods wagons, but in June 1944 it handled 5,246. New sidings had to be built just for the landings at both Micheldever and Brockenhurst. Military passenger traffic was also heavy, with Southampton handling 364,350 British troops between D-day and VE Day, as well as 2,165,883 Americans and 310,113 prisoners of war.

On the Hampshire coast, the small port of Lymington, in peacetime simply the mainland terminus of one of the quietest routes to the Isle of Wight – that to Yarmouth – had its slipways doubled so that two tank-landing craft could be loaded at the same time. Further east in West Sussex, the small port of Littlehampton handled ammunition and the channel port of Newhaven was used as an embarkation port for troops. Newhaven had closed in July 1940, but reopened the following year to handle coal brought by coastal shipping mainly from South Wales. In fact, while the North Sea and Straits of Dover were closed to normal merchant shipping movements, coal shipments by sea increased between South Wales and the Southern Railway ports of Southampton, Newhaven, Fremington, Cowes and Highbridge from their pre-war level of 37,500 tons to a peak of 111,200 tons in 1943. Lymington lacked the facilities to handle coal shipments.

Some idea of the Southern Railway's contribution to the war effort in terms of railway operations alone can be gathered from the fact that, from 3 September 1939 to 8 May 1945, the number of special trains for the government handled by the company amounted to:

Troop trains: 30,890
Troops carried: 9,367,886
Goods trains: 35,360
PoW trains (June 1944–May 1945): 1,127
PoWs carried: 582,005
Ambulance trains: 1,797
Passengers on ambulance trains: 408,051 (including medical staff)
BEF leave trains, 1940: 1,429 with 142,021 personnel
BEF leave trains, Jan–May 1945: 1,746 with 845,940 personnel.

Meanwhile, by 6 December 1944 the launching sites for the V-weapons had been overrun, the Germans no longer had fuel to mount any other form of aerial attack, and evacuees were officially encouraged to return. While there was an initial surge before Christmas, on this occasion the flow homewards was far steadier, increasing after 8 May 1945.

BLITZED

All of the railway companies suffered in the German bomber campaign that followed the Battle of Britain, known popularly as the Blitz, but the Southern also received its share of the attacks that were part of the Battle of Britain and directed against airfields in the south as the Luftwaffe attempted to wipe out the RAF. The first impact on the Southern was as early as 19 June 1940, when bombs destroyed the engineers' works at Redbridge, near Southampton, and destroyed a large quantity of sleepers. On 10 July, a train was bombed near Newhaven, killing the driver and injuring the guard. On 16 August, a bomb blocked two lines at New Malden and killed railwaymen and passengers. This type of incident was to become commonplace as the Blitz on London and other major cities got under way, effectively lasting from September 1940 until May 1941.

Between 24 August 1940 and 10 May 1941, there were raids on some part of the Southern network for 250 out of the 252 days. One of the most serious incidents occurred on 7 September 1940, at Vauxhall, between Clapham Junction and Waterloo, when a high-explosive bomb hit the approaches to Waterloo, penetrating the brick viaduct before exploding and causing so much damage that the station had to be closed. Despite the railway's own resources being reinforced by those of the army, the station could not be reopened until 19 September, and then only partially with just two roads available for traffic. Operations didn't return to normal until 1 October. The running of so many of the approaches to the London termini over viaducts was a serious weakness, with those between Blackfriars and Loughborough Junction damaged in two places by bombs during the Blitz. The line to Herne Hill from Loughborough Junction was also hit twice, with the overbridge carrying the South London Line and Catford loop having a narrow escape.

On 12 October 1940, the Southern's own power station at Durnsford Road was hit by a high-explosive bomb, destroying one of the chimneys and part of the boiler house, so that the station's generating capacity was cut by half. The repairs included erecting a new 100ft-high steel chimney, and could not be completed until 12 February. In the meantime, a parachute mine landed next to the signal cabin at London Bridge on 12 December but did not explode and, as mentioned in Chapter 2, the signalmen continued working while a naval bomb-disposal team defused it. London Bridge was less lucky the next time, as the so-called 'fire raid' on the night of 29/30 December saw the station buildings gutted and the southern side of the Central Section station badly damaged. That night, Waterloo also had to close again for a time because of incendiary bombs.

Victoria, the Southern's other large terminus, was in effect two termini in one. To the west was the former London, Brighton & South Coast Railway terminus, and to the east that of the South East & Chatham Railway. On Christmas Eve 1940, a large bomb had been dropped onto the tracks just outside the Brighton side of the station, missing the signal gantry but possibly doing even more damage by exploding on the track beneath it and lifting the gantry off its foundations with such force that it was actually blown off the railway's land. Rather than replace the gantry with one of identical size and design, as it had been built for semaphore signals and adapted for colour light signals, it was decided to build one of the smallest possible size, both for economy and because of the shortage of materials. Adapting a design used elsewhere and using materials that were already in the factory, the signal manufacturer managed to produce a new gantry ready for delivery in just five days, as opposed to the two months that such work would normally have taken.

At the height of the Blitz, one train arriving from Ramsgate at Charing Cross had been driven through heavy bombing, and at times the two enginemen had been forced to stop and leave their cab to lie flat on their faces to avoid being injured by shrapnel. As they approached Charing Cross, an oil bomb landed in their tender, but they managed to put it out using the engine hose.

A further major raid on the night of 16/17 April 1941 saw a landmine fall on the older part of the Hungerford Bridge, which carried the lines into Charing Cross, while incendiary bombs started fires inside the terminus itself, damaging buildings, platforms and rolling stock. The landmine was welded to the third rail but failed to explode, and fortunately a fire that had started in the bridge timbers was put out just 10ft away from it. Downstream there was far worse, as another high-explosive bomb destroyed the bridge across Southwark Street on the approaches to Blackfriars and Holborn Viaduct, and knocked out the Blackfriars signal cabin. Once again, the Southern's own resources were reinforced by the military, but it took fifteen days to restore two roads, and a new bridge was not completed until 9 October 1942. A temporary signalling arrangement had to be installed.

The final raid on the night of 10/11 May 1941 was one of the worst. Waterloo was damaged by at least fifty-one high-explosive bombs, incendiaries and parachute mines, while the incendiaries started a major fire after they penetrated a spirits store in the arches beneath the terminus. In fact, one unexploded 2,000lb bomb was not discovered until work started on an adjoining office building in 1959. Cannon Street also suffered from bombs and incendiaries, and the locomotive that tried to rescue a van train by pulling it out from under the blazing roof onto the bridge was itself struck by a bomb. Holborn Viaduct was gutted by fires started by incendiary bombs and could not be used until 1 June. At Elephant & Castle, the island platform and up local platforms were burned out, and a temporary up main platform had to be provided before it could reopen on 1 September.

Driver L. Stainer of Bricklayers' Arms recalled the night of 10/11 May:

We stopped the engine at Borough Market and the Fireman put out incendiaries.

On arriving at Cannon Street, Platform 6, bombs began to drop, then the aspect signal lights all went out, and then some bombs dropped outside the station, bringing clouds of dust.

A fire had then started at the side of the station, and it rained bombs and there seemed to be no stopping. The fires were then like huge torches and there were thousands of sparks.

The smoke from the fires blacked out the moon, and fires seemed to be everywhere, and then the station roof caught alight.

To save the trains catching fire, two engines coupled together, No. 934 and 1541, pulled out of Platform 8 on to the bridge. We stopped twenty yards ahead of the other train, and then, after about ten minutes we ducked down on the footplate. We counted three bombs, the last one was terrific and very close. There was a terrific explosion and our engine seemed to roll; at first we thought our train had been hit. The debris flew in all directions – we were very lucky. My fireman said at the time, 'Look out – we are going in the drink,' and I said, 'I thought my back week had come' [sic].

We looked round, and found that the bomb had made a direct hit on the boiler of No. 934 engine, and it had also blasted our train, and turned part of the train over on its side.

My fireman and myself went to see where the driver and fireman were, and I am pleased to say that they had got off the engine in time.

Then, looking around, we found our train had caught fire, and the fireman with buckets of water tried to put same out, but it was impossible as a strong wind was blowing up the Thames, and the fire got the master.

I uncoupled my engine from the train, and drew back about two yards, and scoured the engine, and then crossed to the west of the bridge until dawn, watching the fires. It was just like as if Hell had been let loose.

(*War on the Line*, Southern Railway, London, 1946)

Fortunately, no one was injured and Driver Stainer paid tribute to the coolness of the station staff at Cannon Street.

The damage to Waterloo from the fires among the spirit stores in its basement arches was such that the station was closed until 15 May, and even then it could only reopen partially. Meanwhile, its unfortunate commuters were forced to alight at Clapham Junction, where special buses were meant to take them to Waterloo. The bus service was overwhelmed by the large numbers needing to use it, and at one point the queue for buses stretched for more than a mile. Getting on a bus, overcrowded, was in itself no guarantee of progress as the roads from Clapham Junction were difficult to drive over as they were cluttered with fire hoses as firemen struggled to put out fires.

The worst affected of the Southern Railways' stretches of track were, naturally enough, all on the approaches to the London termini, and of these the most bombs and parachute mines per route mile fell on the 2¼ miles between Waterloo and Queen's Road, with no fewer than ninety-two 'incidents', as the authorities rather coyly described them. Charing Cross and Cannon Street to New Cross and New Cross Gate, 5½ route miles, recorded 123 incidents, while the 4½ route miles from Holborn Viaduct to Herne Hill suffered sixty-two incidents.

London was not alone in receiving the attentions of the Luftwaffe. At Portsmouth, both Portsmouth & Southsea and Portsmouth Harbour stations suffered severe damage from bombing, with considerable loss of rolling stock, including electric multiple units. On the night of 11/12 January 1941, a train including 4 COR main-line electric sets was hit while at platform 4 at Portsmouth Harbour, with the viaduct breached, leaving the train marooned. It was not lifted out by cranes until September 1946.

Under such conditions, the need to keep the rolling stock as safe as possible was a major difficulty. The one place that was ideal for this was Kemp Town Tunnel at Brighton on a stretch of line which had lost its passenger service but the track, fortunately, had been retained for goods services. The tunnel was first used to stable electric stock for a trial three weeks in October 1941, but the practice then became regular and continued until May 1944. The electric multiple units were shunted into and out of the tunnel by steam locomotives. At Bournemouth West, the station was kept open all night so that rolling stock could be moved to safety at short notice.

Once the Blitz was over, the Luftwaffe still mounted many 'hit and run' raids, usually at targets on the south coast as few of these reached London. On 25 May 1943, during a raid on Brighton, a bomb passed through a house and bounced over the garden wall to explode against one of the 70ft-high piers of the London Road Viaduct, bringing down two spans. It took fifteen days to effect temporary repairs and the damage was not completely repaired for four months. In the meantime, passengers between Brighton and Lewes had to make a lengthy diversion via Haywards Heath, although extra trains were operated between Haywards Heath and Lewes for their benefit.

STRAFING AND FLYING BOMBS

Not all of the damage was done by shellfire, bombs or missiles, as the Southern was within even the short range of a German fighter and trains provided a tempting target for a strafing attack. One fine, calm summer's evening, a train was approaching Deal on its run from Ramsgate to Dover, when six German fighters dived out of the sky, deliberately aiming at the locomotive footplate. The crew drew into what shelter they could find, and then at the last moment slammed on the brakes, hoping to make the Germans miss their target and meanwhile jump down onto the track to save themselves. As they jumped, it was clear that the driver had been hit, with a large hole in his chest, and it was clear to the fireman that he was dead. The fireman was wounded in the arm, the thigh, leg and foot, and as he staggered towards the guard, he fainted. Fortunately, the guard had been trained in first aid and was able to use a tourniquet for the fireman's arm, where an artery had been severed, and saved his life. Royal Marines stationed nearby provided assistance, putting out the fire and helping to rescue passengers from the burning train. A light engine came off a train at Deal station and, having obtained permission for wrong-line working, pulled the crippled train back to Walmer.

This was just one of many similar incidents. In one case, when a Guildford to Horsham train was attacked near Bramley, just a few miles south of Guildford, the fireman was the only person on the train not to be injured, while seven passengers were killed.

Any feeling that the return of Allied forces to France meant that the war was ending was soon dispelled when the flying-bomb campaign began in summer 1944. The arrival of a V-1 near Haywards Heath was supposed to have been the first. On 17 June, a V-1 hit a goods train on a bridge between Elephant & Castle and Loughborough Junction. The next day, another wrecked 100ft of the southern end of Hungerford Bridge and, while restricted working resumed on 20 June, full normal working could not resume until 4 December. Further damage occurred at Victoria, Eastern Section, to the terminal platforms at Wimbledon normally used by the District Line, and to Charlton, Falconwood and Forest Hill stations. A bridge on the Quarry Line at Merstham was damaged, shifting its girders, and the main lines at Bricklayers Arms Junction were cut. The bridge carrying the Catford Loop over the South London Line at Peckham Rye was so badly damaged by a V-1 landing alongside on 12 July that it had to be demolished and replaced, giving the Southern's engineers a massive problem since the bridge also carried high-tension cables from the distribution room at Lewisham. The temporary bridge was ready for normal services to resume on 23 July. Another 'near miss' wrecked the signal cabin at Tulse Hill and damaged an underbridge, leading to diversions and cancellations until a temporary signal-box could be brought into use and the bridge repaired on 27 August.

The flying bombs stopped at the end of August, only to be followed by the V-2 rockets, against which there could be no defence and no warning, as winter approached. The colour light signalling on the up side of Hampton Court Junction was put out of action on 2 November, but normal working was restored by 4 November. On 5 November, at Bermondsey, the bridge carrying the up main and local lines and South London lines over Southwark Park Road was hit and collapsed into the road. Again, a temporary bridge had to be provided. Normal working was reinstated late on 14 November, and in the meantime trains had to be cancelled or diverted. A block of flats at Deptford owned by the Southern Railway and accommodating railwaymen and their families was hit by a V-2 in March 1945, with a quarter of the flats demolished and fifty-one people killed.

All in all, the Southern alone had seen fourteen bridges demolished, another forty-two seriously damaged and 143 less seriously damaged. Incidents per 100 route miles on the Southern tell the story, with 170 incidents per 100 route miles compared with thirty-three on the GWR, twenty-nine on the LMS and just twenty-eight on the LNER, despite the latter's lines being in Essex and East Anglia and along the east coast. There were 3,637 incidents on the Southern's 2,135 route miles, whereas the LMS had 1,939 incidents on 6,672 route miles.

WATERLOO & CITY LINE

The only deep-level Tube line owned by a main-line railway, the short Waterloo & City Line linking the Southern Railway's terminus with the City of London at the Bank, without any intermediate stops, had an eventful war. Indeed, for its length it probably had a far higher level of incidents and much lengthier periods of closure than any other Underground line in London.

War stopped deliveries of buses until export vehicles frozen on the outbreak were released to operators at home but, interestingly, the same restrictions were not applied so thoroughly to the railways. Possibly this was because the volume of defence work passing through the railway workshops was enough to curb any massive production of locomotives and rolling stock but, in the event, the Great Western Railway took delivery of its final batch of diesel railcars, and the Southern Railway received its new trains for the Waterloo & City. The work on these trains was too far advanced to be stopped, and the elderly rolling stock that they were to replace had been the subject of not simply complaints, but a passenger pressure group for some years before the war. The new trains were delivered during the spring and early summer of 1940, and entered service on 28 October. New conductor rails were also laid and new signalling installed.

As an isolated Underground railway, the Waterloo & City was seen as being vulnerable to interruptions of the power supply. The Southern reached an agreement with the London Passenger Transport Board for an emergency supply should the W&C's own supply be interrupted.

Before the new trains could be introduced, services were interrupted for a couple of days by a burst water main in the city which sent water flowing into the tunnels, but this was a far less serious event than that which occurred later that year, or the further flooding many years after the war ended. Nevertheless, it showed just how vulnerable the line would be. The London Underground lines running under the River Thames had all been equipped with floodgates before the war, and it had been planned to do the same for the W&C, but this plan was abandoned because of the short length of the track and the fact that it did not inter-connect with any other Tube line.

The W&C operated for most of its life without a Sunday service, and trains did not run on Good Friday or Christmas Day. During the period 1943–7, some services were operated on these 'closed' days for service personnel, easing the pressure on the London Underground system.

War did affect the W&C despite its deep tunnels. On 12 September 1940, the line was closed for twelve hours from 7 a.m. because of an unexploded bomb on the track, presumably at the Waterloo end where a lift existed to move rolling stock to the surface for heavy maintenance. Waterloo main-line station was also experiencing severe difficulties at this time with the approach lines badly damaged by bombing. A month later, on 12 October, Durnsford Road power station was hit by a bomb at 7.16 p.m., which exploded in one of the chimneys, causing it to collapse on the boiler house, destroying half of the boilers. It took four months before they could be replaced. The Southern's extensive surface network survived on current from the National Grid, while the W&C used the facility provided by London Transport. Five days later, on 20 October, at 1.35 a.m., two of the line's sidings at Waterloo were damaged by a bomb, and could not be reopened until 23 October. Bomb damage also caused some further flooding on 9 November.

The worst damage came during the evening of Sunday 8 December 1940, when a 2.200lb bomb penetrated the approach road in the Old Post Office Yard at Waterloo, breaking some 30ft of the crown of the down line which at this point was of cut-and-cover construction near the lift siding. On the surface, the crater was 70ft across. Worse still, water mains were fractured and both tunnels flooded with an estimated 4.5 million gallons of water, which also swept a considerable volume of rubble into the tunnels. Even had the floodgates been fitted, these would not have saved the tunnels because of the location of the water mains. Within two days of the bomb damage, work started on clearing up the mess using outside contractors, but took longer than expected, partly because the damage was much greater and partly because of the wartime shortage of labour. Even with a change of contractor, the Southern had to loan some of its own permanent-way personnel, and instead of resuming a limited, peak-period only, service in February as had been promised, a restricted service did not resume until 3 March 1941, with the full service not reinstated until 15 April. Two days later, the service was again interrupted by another bomb at Waterloo.

While the W&C was closed, the sub-surface booking hall for the Bakerloo and Northern lines was badly damaged on 5 January 1941. This was one means of access to the W&C. An even worse incident occurred at the other end of the line on Saturday 11 January at 7.57 p.m., when a high-explosive bomb crashed through the road into the circular subway under the surface of Bank station, before exploding at the top of the Central Line escalators. Had the W&C still been open, this would have been enough to close the line for some weeks, but it was fortunate that it was a Sunday evening and few people were about as the death toll would have been even higher (see Chapter 11).

A further night of intensive German aerial activity came on 16/17 April 1941, starting at 10.40 p.m. just after the W&C had closed. Bomb damage close to the electricity sub-station at Waterloo caused the current to be cut off and trains could not run the following morning. Nevertheless, once again the emergency supply from the LPTB meant that trains were back in service later that day, until the signal current failed at 1.52 p.m. A temporary closure was also necessary on 19 April while the Royal Navy swept the River Thames for mines. On 10 May, heavy bombing caused serious fires at Waterloo, closing the terminus, and the water used to fight the fires, made worse by the presence of a spirits warehouse under the station, again flooded the W&C sufficiently for the current to have to be cut off. While water was pumped out of the tunnels starting on 11 May, the following day an unexploded bomb was discovered at Bank, and punping could not be restarted until 22 May, before being interrupted again by an unexploded bomb at Walbrook, which blocked access to Bank station, so that normal operations did not resume until 26 May.

A derailment in the terminus at Waterloo, although affecting a surface train, caused the current to be cut off between 7.40 a.m. and 2.25 p.m. on 17 May 1943.

Finally, in December 1943, emergency pumps were installed on the W&C at Waterloo, paid for by the Ministry of War Transport. These were undoubtedly too late to be of any value, although there could have been the possibility of a flying bomb hitting the line's two termini.

ACCIDENTS

In peacetime the Southern was a passenger railway, but in wartime goods trains had priority over everything other than troop trains and ambulance trains. On 4 November 1942, there was thick fog before daybreak and the usual blackout restrictions were in force. The 05.34 from London Bridge to Epsom was standing at Waddon station and could not be passed on to Wallington where shunting was in progress. The delay to the train was so long that, in accordance with the rule book, the guard made his way to the signal-box. While he was there, both the guard and the signalman heard the 06.15 from West Croydon to Holborn Viaduct approaching, but neither could do anything to prevent the ensuing collision in which the 06.15's motorman and a passenger were killed. Even in wartime, attention still had to be paid to safety, and at the official enquiry, the signalman at West Croydon South box maintained that he had received the 'all clear' from Waddon on the Sykes lock-and-block instrument. The implication was that the signalman at Waddon had freed the instrument using his release key in the belief that the 05.34 had departed, but he denied doing so and it seems unlikely that this would have happened with the train's guard present. The inspecting officer suggested installing a system that required signalmen to cooperate, but quite how this could be done was never resolved.

ROMNEY, HYTHE & DYMCHURCH

While the Romney, Hythe & Dymchurch Light Railway was not part of the Southern Railway, it had been built with the support of that company, which felt that the line had a greater chance of success than a heavy rail line across the same area. The RH&D did in any case link in with two Southern branches.

The RH&D was never a toy railway, although its narrow gauge of 15 inches and the scaled model appearance of its tender locomotives give that impression, as opposed to the sturdy tank locomotives favoured by the Welsh narrow-gauge railways. It was a rarity in that it was built for passenger traffic rather than goods. It was the only British narrow-gauge line to become actively involved in the war effort, even though it was not covered by the Emergency (Railway Control) Order of 1939. As with the main-line railways and London Transport, the RH&D not only provided transport for the military, it also handled war work in its workshops and came under enemy attack.

After the fall of France when the south coast appeared to be a likely landing place for a German invasion, the RH&D was handed over to the Royal Engineers, who were at that time the British Army's experts on railway operation. The line was needed to serve troops and gun emplacements spread along the coast, and was soon running troop trains with as many as twenty-one carriages, which could accommodate up to 224 men. In addition, the Royal Engineers constructed an armoured train consisting of the 4–8–2 locomotive *Hercules*, and two bogie hopper wagons, each with a machine gun and an anti-tank rifle. The locomotive was probably chosen for the armoured train as it was one of two constructed for a projected extension that was never built, but which would have involved a steep gradient, while the rest of the RH&D's stud of locomotives were intended to operate along the almost perfectly flat line.

As plans were laid for the Allied invasion of Normandy, Dungeness became the point at which the cross-Channel petrol line, 'Pluto', would be assembled. The RH&D's rolling stock was modified to carry coils of the Pluto pipeline, on which preliminary assembly had taken place in the company's workshops at New Romney and Dungeness. This work started in 1942 and continued until just after the invasion in June 1944.

On one occasion, the line was bombed and a train consisting of a locomotive and nine carriages fell into the crater before it could stop.

MINED

Travel by sea was extremely limited in wartime, with few routes open. One that remained operational with a skeleton service was that between Portsmouth and Ryde on the Isle of Wight. Early in the morning of 20 September 1941, the paddle steamer *Portsdown* was lost after she struck a mine, with eight out of her crew of just eleven killed along with twelve passengers. One of the survivors was the lookout man, Jupe. He recalled:

> We left Portsmouth Harbour Pier at 4 a.m. and I took up my position as lookout in the bows of the *Portsdown*. After we had cleared the outer harbour Channel buoys I reported this to Captain Chandler on the bridge and the vessel was then rounded up to go through the swashway to continue our journey to Ryde. About a minute after this, and before the vessel had completed her alteration of course, I heard a sort of scraping noise along the port side of the ship, and then, after what must have been a few seconds, there was a terrific explosion. At this moment I was looking out across the port bow and I was thrown into the sea. When I came to the surface I grasped a piece of floating wood and swam to the after port sponson, when I climbed on board and assisted in getting out the life boats, both of which were lowered and loaded with passengers'.

(War on the Line, Southern Railway, London, 1946)

Another seventeen passengers were rescued by a boat launched by the Royal Navy.

WARTIME PRODUCTION

The 'Rhino' pontoon sections of the famous Mulberry Harbours for the D-day landings were built in the King George V graving dock at Southampton, just one of many contributions to the war effort with many of the workshops turned over to war production as part of the 'shadow' factory network, often building components for armaments manufacturers, especially at Eastleigh and Ashford. The pressures of wartime saw Brighton works back in production, building thirty locomotives in 1943, while personnel rose from 253 men in 1939 to 755 men, 214 women working full-time and thirty-eight working part-time by the end of

1943. One of the orders handled by Ashford works was the construction in 1941 of 1,000 open 13-ton freight wagons for the USSR, dispatched in sections to the Middle East and reaching their destination through Persia. The works also built bridge components for the LMS and parts for howitzers. Eastleigh built bomb trolleys, parts for aircraft and Matilda tanks, as well as complete landing craft and tailplanes for Horsa troop-carrying gliders. Lancing built stampings for gun breech mechanisms, ambulance trains and wagons.

The marine workshops at Southampton handled repairs and refits to 184 warships, 723 merchant ships and maintenance of water ambulances. Those at Newhaven handled 603 warships, 140 merchant ships, ten hospital carriers and twenty-one RAF high-speed launches. The workshops at Dover, with their Southern Railway personnel, were taken over by the Admiralty on 1 July 1940 and retained until 31 January 1945, keeping warships based at the port in fighting condition.

CHAPTER 11

KEEPING THE HOME FIRES BURNING

While much of its network was further away from the Luftwaffe's airfields than that of the Southern Railway, the Great Western not only ran into London, but also served many other cities that were to prove to be targets, such as Birmingham, Bristol and Plymouth. Bath may have seemed an unlikely target, but the so-called 'Baedeker Raids' put the city on the list. While passenger traffic was very important to the Great Western, it was, by a smaller margin than the LMS and LNER, nevertheless primarily a freight railway, with freight traffic accounting for 58 per cent of turnover before the war. Wartime pressures might not have affected its London commuters so much as there were relatively few of them, and it may indeed have had more commuters in the Birmingham area, but the railway was affected in other ways. The need to keep the coal moving from the pithead to power stations, factories, railway locomotive depots and, bottom of the list by far, homes, placed it under considerable strain. The irony was that the Great Western had designed and built its locomotives to run on the best-quality Welsh steam coal, but in wartime, when maximum performance and more was required, the quality of coal could not be guaranteed.

Elsewhere, while the Great Western ran a train from its evacuation station at Ealing Broadway every ten minutes between 1 and 4 September 1940, its main-line services were reduced to just eighteen trains from Paddington between 8.40 a.m. and 6.35 p.m., with those to the West Country all being routed the 'long way round' via Bristol. Many goods trains were stopped during the period of the evacuation, with few, if any, operating on 1 and 2 September. While the 'Phoney War' persisted, the New Year started badly, with many trains cancelled in what the company magazine proclaimed as the 'Worst Winter Ever', as heavy falls of snow blocked lines and trapped trains.

Despite the reductions in services, a sense of normality seemed to be in the air when the Great Western launched its 1940 edition of *Holiday Haunts* early in the year. At the stations, however, the bright posters extolling the virtues of the many resorts on the Great Western, and on other railways, were soon to be replaced by stern messages from the Ministry of War Transport, demanding to know 'Is your journey really necessary?' The Railways Executive Committee did its bit to discourage travel, raising fares in May 1940 by 10 per cent, both to discourage travel and to cover the mounting costs of the railways. This was to be a constant conflict between the authorities and the public at Christmas and the New Year, and in the summer months during the war years. A war-weary and bomb-battered population would do all it could to get away for a summer holiday, while the authorities made it as difficult for them as possible. At Christmas, people working away from home were anxious to get back for a day or two. To try to help, the armed forces eventually refused to issue forces leave passes at peak periods, which was harsh if the individuals concerned were about to be posted abroad. It must have been with considerable delight on the part of the government that later in the war travel to resorts on the south coast was banned in preparation for the Normandy landings.

In common with the other companies, the Great Western provided ships from its fleet of ferries and cargo vessels to move the BEF to France, and then to help bring it home again, at the cost of severe disruption to its ferry services across the Irish Sea from Fishguard in west Wales to Rosslare, Waterford and Cork, and from Weymouth to the Channel Islands. Indeed, sailings from Weymouth were banned at the outbreak of war. It also provided its share of the trains needed to move the BEF away from the Channel ports, providing forty. For this operation, a problem arose with finding sufficient locomotives capable of running over Southern metals, especially since the route from Reading to the Channel ports was far from being a masterpiece of railway engineering. Most of the locomotives used were 2–6–0s and 'Manor' class 4–6–0s. The trains with the troops from Dunkirk joined the Great Western Railway at Reading, having taken the all-important cross-country Southern Railway North Downs line bypassing the London area for those being taken to Wales, the West Country and the Midlands.

RESTRICTIONS

In common with the other companies, the Great Western operated longer trains during the war years, although it often limited the trains to sixteen carriages, rather than the twenty or more that were often found elsewhere. This led to difficulties. On one occasion, in the blackout, an army private, not realising that this method of working was in force, stepped out of one of the rear carriages of a sixteen-coach train at Bath, and had an unexpected, and no doubt unwanted, ducking in the River Avon. The very long trains used elsewhere did have the disadvantage that time had to be spent dividing them on arrival, so that their carriages could be put into two platforms, with the reverse happening on depart-ure, the front half being drawn clear of the station and then reversed onto the back half.

Often journeys were delayed by the need for heavy trains to be given banking assistance, usually requiring a stop while the banker was coupled and then later uncoupled.

Wartime enforced many other changes, and through working of trains to and from the Metropolitan Line ended on 16 September 1939, by which time emergency cuts were being made to timetables.

Shipping services did not escape the cuts. After helping in the evacuation of those civilians who wished to leave the Channel Islands, services to the islands were abandoned once the Germans invaded. On the Irish Sea, just one ship was left to work the Fishguard and Rosslare route, so that the service was reduced to a frequency of three times a week in each direction. The Fishguard–Waterford service was maintained by the steamer *Great Western*, again initially at a frequency of three times a week in each direction, but this was cut back to twice weekly in August 1940 after a large minefield was sown by the Royal Navy as a defensive measure off the south coast of the Irish Republic. As a further security measure, since many in the UK and in Ireland believed that southern Ireland could be used as a stepping stone for an invasion of Great Britain, the harbour at Waterford was closed during the hours of darkness. The Waterford service was suspended from April 1944, so that the *Great Western* could be taken up from trade for the Normandy landings. As we will see later, the remaining Irish Sea steam packet on the Fishguard–Rosslare service, the *St Patrick*, was to meet an unfortunate end.

Some wartime pressures had to be accommodated by investment in improved facilities. With the Port of London crippled by enemy bombing and by the unacceptable risk from attack for shipping in the Straits of Dover and the Thames estuary, other ports became more important, including those on the Bristol Channel. South Wales was also a major area for the production of coal, steel and iron. This put pressure on the railway system as new traffic flows had to be accommodated. In 1941, the Ministry of War Transport gave authority for the conversion of a 6-mile length of line from Lansdown Junction at Cheltenham to Engine Shed Junction at Gloucester from double to quadruple track. This stretch of line was owned 50:50 by the GWR and the LMS, and it was agreed that the latter would do the construction work and the GWR would lay the track and provide the signalling. Starting in September, the work required considerable land drainage because of the low-lying ground before the embankments could be built.

Expansion in one area during wartime also meant that there had to be cuts elsewhere. All of the grouped railways were extremely reluctant to close lines, but the Railway Executive Committee was made of sterner stuff. It had to be. Every ton of coal consumed, every mile of track used, had to prove its worth. One of the first closures was the line that had started life as the Van Railway, operated by the Cambrian Railway before the grouping. This 6½-mile line had been built to serve a lead mine, and was closed on 4 November 1940. Again at the bidding of the REC, in early 1940 the GWR took over the Weston, Clevedon & Portishead Light Railway, simply to close it on 18 May.

Meanwhile, the new chief mechanical engineer, Frederick Hawksworth, had broken with past GWR tradition and increased the degree of superheating on the latest batch of 'Hall' class locomotives, obtaining a vastly improved performance. The significance of this during wartime was that superheating became even more important when the railways could no longer choose the best South Wales coal. Before this, however, the Ministry of War Transport had decreed that all locomotive production from December 1941 onwards would be of the LMS Stanier 2–8–0 design, and the GWR works at Swindon built eighty of these. The choice of design was influenced by War Office requirements for locomotives capable of handling heavy goods trains.

When the War Office demanded locomotives for service overseas, however, instead of the new austerity 2–8–0 locomotives, troops in North Africa were surprised to see six ex-GWR 0–6–0 Dean goods engines, including one that had served with the War Office in France and Germany during the First World War. The result was that instead of handling heavy military trains during the North African campaign, the former GWR locomotives spent most of their time either shunting or on banking and pilot duties. While one of the locomotives was named *Wavell*, after the general, before departure, unofficially the remaining five locomotives gained girls' names, although whether these were those of sweethearts left at home, nurses at the nearby military hospital or, as one account would have it, ladies of the night at another establishment, could never be confirmed.

Swindon, like the other railway company workshops, had to produce and repair locomotives while also playing its part in war work. Guns and gun mountings were produced at Swindon, as well as shells, ball-bearings, bridges and landing craft. Possibly Swindon was more adaptable than the workshops for other companies, as even before the war its 'product range' had not simply covered almost everything that a railway company might want, but included the production of artificial limbs as well. It was scarcely surprising that the availability and reliability of Great Western locomotives and carriages began to suffer. Rolling stock was also lost to other wartime requirements, such as ambulance trains, fire-fighting trains, and even a mobile canteen train.

UNDER ATTACK

The wartime railways had to continue to serve the nation and provide numerous special trains of one kind or another amid heavy aerial bombardment. In any modern war, the transport system is one of the most important targets, for it not only allows the swift reinforcement of the front line, but also conveys essential supplies, raw materials and, of course, fuel.

At the height of the Blitz on 13 October 1940, there was a near miss at Paddington, but Praed Street station on the Circle Line received a direct hit from a high-explosive bomb and the air-raid precaution services at Paddington were sent down to help. On another night, a bomb fell among lorries parked outside Paddington goods station, wrecking eighteen lorries and sending a handcart flying out of the station to land in the Grand Union Canal.

Paddington was hit several times during the war. A parachute mine demolished part of the departure side of the building in 1941, but the event that caused most disruption to services was early in the morning on a Wednesday in March 1944, when two 1,100lb high-explosive bombs and an incendiary bomb hit the station. The first of the high-explosive bombs pierced the road by platform 11, while the second exploded on platforms

6 and 7, creating a crater 40ft in diameter. Debris damaged platforms 3, 4 and 8, while 5, 6 and 7 were out of use. Nevertheless, by 5 p.m. platform 5 was back in use, and twenty-four hours later so too was platform 8. Later that same year, a V-1 flying bomb damaged the roof and platforms 6 and 7, but traffic was not disrupted for long. There were many other incidents, although with a network that lay to the west of London and in Wales, the GWR was probably the least badly hit by aerial attack of any of the 'Big Four'.

While the incident involving a trainload of bombs at Soham in Cambridgeshire on the LNER was due to a fault with a wagon, at Birkenhead on the GWR it was enemy action that caused what was potentially a major incident with another train carrying bombs. An air raid on Birkenhead and Liverpool involved the Luftwaffe dropping both high-explosive and incendiary bombs. Norman Tunna, a shunter in the Great Western marshalling yard was continuing to work through the raid, and had just marshalled a goods train of high-explosive bombs, which was ready to leave. Such trains always had their contents covered by a waterproof sheet so that they would not be revealed. As he walked along the train making a final check, Tunna saw a wagon full of 250lb bombs with its waterproof covering sheet ablaze. He quickly went to the locomotive for a bucket of water, but this had no effect at all on the fire. He quickly tore off the sheet hoping that the incendiaries would come with it, while the driver and firemen hastened to him with further buckets of water. One of the incendiaries came away with the sheet, but the other fell between two bombs inside the wagon. Water had little or no effect on incendiaries, but the spray from the stirrup pump worked by one of the two enginemen did at least keep the bombs cool. Meanwhile, Tunna jumped into the wagon and prised the two bombs apart, releasing the incendiary, which he picked up and threw out of the wagon. He then joined the enginemen in spraying the bombs in the wagon until he judged that they were cool enough to be safe.

Norman Tunna was one of three railwaymen to be awarded the George Cross – the other two being the two LNER enginemen at Soham.

The so-called 'Baedeker raids' of April to June 1944 had as their objective the destruction of many cities without significant strategic importance, and as far as the GWR was concerned, this included Bath and Exeter.

Bath was treated not to a single night of bombing, but to two successive nights. West of the city centre, the line to Bristol was hit in no fewer than nine places. The most serious of these was to the 30ft-high retaining wall carrying the line above and alongside the Lower Bristol Road, which was demolished for 100ft in length, leaving the up railway line hanging in mid-air. The down line was also damaged, but it was decided that this could be made safe by inserting longitudinal timbers, and with crossover points at each side of the breach the line could be worked as a single track section past the damage. Repairs to the up line meant building a temporary bridge to carry the line over the breach in the wall.

At Exeter, the new GWR divisional superintendent maintained that the night of bombing there was more intense than anything he had experienced during the London Blitz. This was part of the problem for those facing the 'Baedeker raids'. The towns chosen were far smaller in size than London and the damage tended to be more concentrated. Even the seaside resorts were not immune, and Weston-super-Mare was subjected to a raid using incendiaries in early summer, doubtless aimed at those taking an early summer break, something all too rare and too brief in wartime.

While the GWR had its share of bombs on its tracks, in its marshalling yards, works and stations, an incident that stands out was the bombing of the Falmouth branch in 1941. The bomb cratered the track before the driver of locomotive No. 4510 had a chance to stop, and the train of three carriages was derailed. Unlike Weston-super-Mare or Bath, Falmouth was an obvious target area, with extensive ship repair facilities and one of the world's largest and best anchorages, as well as being located on the Western Approaches. Ships disabled on transatlantic convoy duty could be saved if they reached Falmouth.

At Plymouth, No. 4911 *Bowden Hall* was destroyed by a direct hit from a bomb. This was just one of many such incidents, and although true direct hits on locomotives were rare and usually the result of bad luck, many more were damaged beyond repair by near misses or by running onto bomb-damaged track before they could be stopped.

The ability of the railways to keep the country moving at the height of the Blitz was due in part to their own extensive engineering facilities and the accepted standard that, whenever there had been a peacetime accident, the priority was to clear the wreckage, repair any damage to track and signals, and get trains moving again as quickly as possible. Those who have experienced the time taken for the recovery of services after accidents in recent years would find this hard to comprehend.

These capabilities had been enhanced by the funds made available before the war by the companies and the government to prepare for wartime.

One example of what could be achieved on the Great Western was when a high-explosive bomb fell on a steel viaduct at midnight, damaging the main lines, a major supporting girder and some of the cross girders. Within a few hours, one line was reopened. Even when a bomb fell on track away from bridges and viaducts, damage was severe, as when a stick of three high-explosive bombs hit a section of main line between Slough and Paddington and damaged all four lines, leaving large craters. Within two hours, the craters had been filled with earth and rubble, while another two hours saw the two least-damaged lines restored to traffic, and all four lines were opened four hours after that.

In extreme cases, the Royal Engineers could be called upon to help the railway company personnel, which was a fair exchange given that many employees had been members of special territorial units of the RE in peacetime and were no doubt doing sterling work in army uniform.

The Great Western invited its staff to hit back after the Battle of Britain by establishing its own 'Spitfire Fund', to raise £5,000 to pay for an aircraft. To get the fund off to a good start, the directors donated the first £500.

While the Normandy landings had persuaded many that the war was all but over, the flying-bomb campaign with first the V-1s and then the V-2s meant that peace seemed far away for those in London and the south-east. Nevertheless, restrictions on lighting on trains and at stations were eased from October 1944, with an interim level known as the 'dim out', and station name boards started to be returned to their normal positions.

The big problem was that despite a restricted train service, commuter traffic actually increased in wartime as many of the more affluent Londoners moved to the outer suburbs or even further out to escape the worst of the bombing. For holidays and for evacuees, the west of England and Wales were seen as the best options, not least because most of the south coast was taken over for military purposes. The east coast resorts were not much better off. On the morning of 29 July 1944, a summer Saturday, Paddington was closed for three hours, and no Underground tickets were sold to Paddington, because the main concourse and platforms were blocked solid with people waiting to catch trains. The problems of wartime had been compounded by government restrictions on extra trains and even on extra carriages on existing trains, adding to the much reduced frequencies and extended journey times. It took three telephone calls by the general manager, Sir James Milne, to the Ministry of War Transport, and the threat of a visit to Downing Street, before a man from the ministry arrived and authorised the use of the locomotives and carriages that were standing idle at Old Oak Common depot. The restrictions were eased somewhat after this, but even so, at August bank holiday weekend, then taken early in August, mounted police had to be called in and the queues snaked along Eastbourne Terrace, which did at least have the advantage of allowing passengers to get to and from the trains.

There was disruption of a different kind on 16 October 1944. The locomotive of a down empty carriage train was derailed outside Paddington close to the parcels depot. This was soon followed by two coaches of the down 'Cornish Riviera' express being derailed at the same point, and although there were no casualties, the line was blocked and normal working could not resume until the following morning.

Overall, the GWR had not had a bad war, although it had lost a number of locomotives to the war effort with these being posted overseas. Its total of thirty-three incidents per 100 route miles compared very well with the Southern Railway's record of 170, but it was higher than the twenty-nine on the LMS and just twenty-eight on the LNER, despite the latter's lines in Essex and East Anglia and up the east coast being that much closer to the bases for German bombers.

Wartime traffic showed some considerable increases. On the Birmingham–Cardiff route, where diesel railcars were operated in multiple for the first time with a corridor coach between them to provide what would now be known as a three-car diesel multiple unit or DMU, traffic was so buoyant that this had to be replaced by a steam locomotive and six or more carriages. Some progress was made with higher capacity goods vehicles. At the outbreak of the Second World War, the GWR already had many six-wheeled oil wagons, and its oil-carrying capacity was boosted during the war by the arrival of eight-wheeled bogie oil wagons from the United States. These carried 40 tons of oil. The barrels and the bogies were shipped as dismantled units and assembled by the Great Western after arrival in the UK. Despite the air of austerity and the difficulties of wartime operation, some peacetime traffic persisted, with the annual harvest of broccoli from Cornwall to London and the

Midlands, a new traffic that had only dated from 1925, growing from 41,474 tons in 1938 to more than 50,000 tons by 1943.

Nevertheless, not all was well, and one of the problems that emerged during the war years and which became worse as the war progressed was what the company described as 'pilferage' on its system. Unfortunately, the blackout had made criminal activity easier, whether planned or simply opportunistic. It was also true that wartime shortages tempted many who in easier circumstances would never have dreamed of stealing – consignments of food and clothing were most at risk.

ACCIDENTS

As a fuller understanding of the implications of working a railway in wartime dawned on those involved, many were thankful that the main Great Western express locomotives had been fitted with speedometers, as in the blackout picking up those points of reference that would give an experienced driver an idea of his speed was to become so difficult as to be almost impossible. Indeed, in the accident at Norton Fitzwarren all the evidence suggests that the driver had either become completely disorientated or was exhausted and stressed for understandable personal reasons, and quite possibly both. Between the wars, and indeed even before the grouping, the Great Western had been the most safety conscious of all the railways, pioneering automatic train control with a system that did not simply warn the driver of danger ahead, but also reassured him that all was well.

Even without automatic train protection, railway lines were protected by track circuits, which coordinated the workings of home and distant signals, and of signals and points. The result was that a train could not enter a block section until the train in front had passed the distant signal, actuated the track circuit and then passed clear of the following home signal. Further interlocking meant that a signalman could not lower a starting signal to allow a train to run to the next signal-box along the line until the signalman in that box had accepted the train and pegged his instrument to 'line clear'.

Nevertheless, there were weaknesses in the system, especially if a starting signal was not linked to the following distant signal by a track circuit. The system was complicated by a railway that had to accommodate slow and heavy coal trains among fast-running expresses, as on the main line between South Wales and London, necessitating many passing loops. In common with most automatic safety systems, the GWR's automatic train control warning system allowed the locomotive driver to cancel a warning, retaining full control of the train if he decided that an emergency brake application was unnecessary.

On the night of 4 November 1940, the driver of an overnight passenger train from Paddington to the west of England was routed onto the down relief line as he was running late. On the GWR, drivers sat on the right-hand side of the cab, unlike the other railway companies, and the driver of this train thought that the signals on the main line, set at 'clear' for a down newspaper train, were for his train, while the signals for the relief line were set at danger. When the alarm sounded in his cab, he cancelled the warning and continued towards the station. As he approached Norton Fitzwarren station, 2 miles west of Taunton, the newspaper train began to overhaul his train and the two trains passed as they ran through the station. Only then did the driver of the passenger train realise his mistake and apply the brakes. The main line and the relief line converged at points on the west side of the station, where the main line was protected by a trap point that took the relief line into a dead end with soft ground on the other side. With the relief-line signals set at danger, the trap point took the passenger train towards the end of the line, and while the driver was braking hard there was not enough room for him to stop, and his 'King' class locomotive, No. 6028 *King George VI*, ploughed into the soft ground and six of the carriages behind it were derailed, scattering over the tracks.

As with most wartime trains, there was severe overcrowding, with an estimated 900 passengers on the train, of whom twenty-seven were killed and another seventy-five injured, fifty-six of them seriously.

The newspaper train escaped, but only just and probably only by virtue of its much higher speed. The paintwork of the last coach was scraped and bits of wreckage from the passenger train flew into the guard's van.

While the driver of the passenger train was at fault, the accident was caused in part by the difficulties of working in the blackout. The driver's house had also been damaged in bombing only two days earlier, so in this case criticism by the accident inspector was far less severe than would have been the case otherwise.

There were also mitigating circumstances for the other accident on the Great Western in wartime. In 1943, the 'British Railways' were presented with additional locomotive power from across the Atlantic with the loan of 2–8–0 American locomotives. The 'loan' was in fact very short, as the following year, as the Allies advanced through Europe, these locomotives were taken back again. While built to the British loading gauge, the locomotives were prepared for service on British metals by the Great Western Railway at Swindon, but were operated in a pool so that they could easily be made available to whichever company needed them at the time. In November 1943, one of these locomotives was on loan to the Great Western, working an overnight freight train from Banbury to Margam in South Wales, running through Leamington, Stratford-upon-Avon and Cheltenham, with a crew change at Leamington and then a further change at Stratford, in complete contrast to the GWR's pre-war practice. The three different crews' lack of familiarity with the locomotive seems to have been a factor in the accident.

On the American locomotives, the layout of the controls was similar to that on the Great Western, with the locomotives being 'right-hand drive' rather than left-hand as on the other British railways. The water gauge again followed GWR practice being on the left-hand side, convenient for the fireman to keep an eye on it. The test cocks, of which there were three – steam, water and drain – were on the driver's side, but differed from those used by railways in Britain by having wheel-operated screw-valve cocks rather than the plug type. This was important because the British plug type showed immediately by the position of the handle whether the valve was open or closed, but the American valves could only be shown as open or closed by feel. A warning notice was placed in the cab by the steam valve warning footplatemen of the difference.

The Leamington crew checked the water gauge on taking over, but as the locomotive headed towards Stratford-upon-Avon, the fireman noticed an unusual swirling or bubbling of the water in the glass, and pointed this out to his driver. The driver mentioned the problem to the next crew when they changed over at Stratford-upon-Avon, but the third driver didn't notice a problem after he had tested the gauge. Seven miles into the next stage of the journey, steaming at around 25mph on a rising gradient, the firebox crown collapsed, scalding the fireman, although in the darkness neither the victim nor the driver realised how seriously. The locomotive stopped, and the fireman walked a mile to Honeybourne East signal-box to raise the alarm before collapsing. Despite the signalman being an experienced ambulance man, thanks to the GWR's safety movement between the wars, the fireman died of his injuries the following day.

Tests after the accident found that the American steam gauge showed a false water level if the gauge was not opened sufficiently. When the tests were repeated from the second crew, they confirmed that this had been the phenomenon that they had noted during their spell on the footplate.

TRAGEDY AT SEA

Many feared that the Irish Sea service was vulnerable to attack by U-boats, although the last steam packet remaining on the service did attempt to steam fast enough to make herself a difficult target. Nevertheless, despite the considerable distance from enemy airfields, it was the Luftwaffe that was to account for the *St Patrick*. *St Patrick* was one of the ships operated by the Fishguard & Rosslare Railway & Harbour Company, a 50:50 partnership between the GWR and the Great Southern Railway of Ireland.

On the morning of 13 June 1941, the *St Patrick* was heading for Fishguard and was only 25 miles from the port when she was surprised by a solitary German bomber and attacked. The first that many of those aboard knew of the attack was the sound of an explosion and the lights going out. The ensuing fire soon went out of control and destroyed a number of the ship's lifeboats. One of the stewardesses, Miss May Owen, was in charge of the after cabin in the third-class section of the ship, where she was responsible for ten women and two children. Six of the women and a child were in the upper section of the cabin, while four women and the other child were in the lower section. As soon as she heard the explosion, May Owen shepherded the passengers in the upper section of the cabin on deck, and then went to find those in the lower section, but as the ship was already listing heavily, the cabin door was jammed. It took several attempts before she could force the cabin door open, and inside in the darkness she found one of the passengers having hysterics while the others were searching for their luggage. She somehow managed to get them out of the cabin and up to the boat deck.

There was more chaos on the boat deck, but another steward took charge of three of the women and the child, putting them in the one undamaged lifeboat, while May Owen attempted to calm the hysterical passenger. Nevertheless, time was running out and as the ship began to slide under the waves, it was essential not to be caught too close to it and be sucked under. The hysterical woman passenger had lost her lifebelt in the escape from the cabin, but May Owen managed to get her over the rail and both women jumped into the sea. After trying to grab her rescuer by the neck, fortunately the passenger lost consciousness, but May Owen then had to keep her afloat for two hours before they could be hauled aboard a life raft. For her courage, May Owen was awarded the George Medal and the Lloyds War Medal.

The radio operator had also done his duty, finding his way in the dark to his wireless room and using an emergency transmitter to send an SOS and position before the room itself was flooded. The destroyer HMS *Wolsey* and a minesweeper picked up the signal. They arrived to find many of the survivors covered with oil from the ship's bunkers.

The human cost was heavy. The *St Patrick* had been carrying a crew of forty-five and the same number of passengers. The master and seventeen crew members perished, as well as twelve passengers.

CHAPTER 12

REPLACING THE COASTERS

On the outbreak of war, the London & North Eastern Railway was probably the most impoverished of the 'Big Four' main-line railways. It had the distinction of holding the world speed record for steam traction – one that persists to this day – with the 126 miles per hour achieved by the sleek Gresley 4–6–2 A4 Pacific *Mallard* in 1938. Yet at the other end of the scale, it missed the chance to electrify its busy suburban routes out of London's Liverpool Street, something that would even have been extended to Clacton had the network belonged to the Southern Railway, and although work started, it was delayed by the war and did not finish until after nationalisation. Its great weakness lay in poor procurement. In contrast to the Great Western where standardisation was seen as a priority, the LNER thought of 'horses for courses' and built even its magnificent express locomotives in small batches. As for its locomotives for branch lines, commuter work and goods, it built relatively few of these, although its 2–6–2 V2 class was to come to be regarded as one of the best.

Part of the LNER's problem was that it was three different railways. There were the long-distance services from King's Cross running to Edinburgh and further north to Aberdeen on the one hand, while on the other there were the services from Liverpool Street which included substantial suburban traffic, as well as the medium-distance traffic to Cambridge and King's Lynn, or to Clacton and Norwich, with the busy Southend line falling in between. It was the railway most dependent upon freight traffic, and especially so in the north of England and Scotland. The third element were the services from London's small Marylebone station, the last terminus to be built in the metropolis, and which had relatively light traffic during peacetime. Unlike today, however, Marylebone's services reached as far north as Manchester.

As with the other railway companies, the London & North Eastern Railway played its part in the mass evacuation of children from London and the other main industrial centres. One of its two embarkation points was New Barnet station, not perhaps the most convenient as children had travelled from their homes to Enfield West station, now renamed Oakwood, on the Piccadilly Line, and then boarded buses for the few miles to New Barnet. Waiting for them were suburban carriages with a few main-line carriages gathered from other routes, with no more than a skeleton service for the regular travellers. The use of outer suburban stations was partly to avoid congestion in the central area, but also recognised the fact that war was expected to break out at any moment, and many believed that it would do so without formal declaration and with a massive air raid.

The LNER's other major evacuee handling point was at Stratford, on the lines from Liverpool Street. That the operation was such a success was due in no small part to an LNER man, Sir Ralph Wedgwood, chairman of the Railway Executive Committee, and until his retirement in March 1939, general manager of the LNER.

The LNER was more than any other a freight railway, which may well have been one reason for its inter-war poverty. On the one hand, there were its crack Anglo-Scottish expresses and its heavy commuter traffic, especially into Liverpool Street, and its boat trains for passengers to the Netherlands, or even its string of seaside resorts in East Anglia, Lincolnshire and Yorkshire, promoted as being the 'drier side of Britain'. On the other, its health and wealth were determined by the coal mines of Yorkshire, Durham, Northumberland and the east of Scotland, by the agricultural traffic of East Anglia, fish from East Anglia and Humberside, and by the manufacturing industries of eastern England and the east of Scotland. In wartime, it was soon to be discovered that, after the fall of Denmark and Norway, and then the Low Countries, the east coast would be untenable for coastal shipping and the bulk of this traffic was to be transferred to the railways.

Having had experience of German bombing of London and east-coast towns during the First World War, when one of its predecessor companies, the Great Eastern, had been targeted twice by German bombing at Liverpool Street, the LNER expected to suffer greatly. The first of the earlier bombing raids had caused considerable disruption to services for a brief period, and the second saw serious damage to an express waiting to depart for Hunstanton. Oddly, the other predecessor companies, the Great Northern at King's Cross and the Great Central at Marylebone, were left untouched during the First World War. While the LNER suffered greatly in the London area, it escaped relatively lightly elsewhere, despite its closer proximity to German airbases, even though both Sheffield and Hull suffered from heavy bombing.

Given its lack of standardised freight and mixed-traffic locomotives, the one really suitable class that was available was the V2 class 2–6–2. The company did benefit considerably when private owners' wagons were requisitioned, although compensation for this had to come from the LNER share of the funds made available by a parsimonious Treasury.

As elsewhere, the outbreak of war was followed by severe cuts to railway passenger services, partly to save fuel and manpower, but also in anticipation of immediate heavy bombing. These cuts were common to all of the railway companies and were far too severe. On 11 September 1939, the LNER issued a new timetable, cutting crack expresses and introducing trains that could at best be described as 'semi-fast' in their place. The public uproar was such that the Railways Executive Committee relented, and on 2 October a new timetable showing improved services was published. Even so, there were fewer trains and these were all slower than those for the same period of the previous year, while amenities such as restaurant cars were missing, and there were just three sleeping car trains. The 'Flying Scotsman' was replaced by a 10 a.m. service to Edinburgh that did not reach its destination until 7.30 p.m., adding three hours to the pre-war schedule. Performance was not helped by lengthy refreshment stops, such as fifteen minutes at Grantham and eighteen minutes at Peterborough, needed to compensate for the lack of catering facilities on the trains. This was a backward step, to the early days of railway travel, before dining cars appeared. The cuts at King's Cross were as nothing to those at Marylebone, with just two Manchester trains a day and these taking six hours forty minutes for the journey, and no fast trains out of the station between 10 a.m. and 5 p.m. No doubt the services from Manchester were seen as expendable, except for traffic to and from intermediate stations, as the city was also served by the LMS from Euston. Throughout the railway system, scheduling was not helped by a 60mph maximum speed restriction.

Despite the looming shortage of everything, including paper, yet another new timetable was issued on 4 December, with more trains and with the return of a number of restaurant and buffet cars; the refreshment stops were also much reduced.

The LNER probably suffered the most from the demands of the British Army for railway locomotives, despite its own limited resources. The Ministry of Supply moved quickly to take the company's ex-Great Central 2–8–0 locomotives, which were seen as ideal for heavy goods and troop train operation, and these went to France with the British Expeditionary Force in 1939. Needless to say, the locomotives in France were lost to the German push through the Low Countries and into France, which was doubly unfortunate as the LNER bore the brunt of the so-called 'convoy coal trains' which started in February 1940, initially to restock coal supplies after the severe disruption of December 1939 and January 1940, but then also to compensate for the loss of a shipping service along the east coast.

BRAVERY ON THE LINE

The air war did not take long to reach the LNER, and Liverpool Street was an early casualty, being badly damaged by bombing soon after the start of the Blitz on 7 September 1940. The raid resulted in several bombs falling on the station, exploding on platforms 1 and 4, with the former wrecking a train completely, so that it took several days to clear. Platform 18 was also damaged at the concourse end and the booking office also suffered. An unexploded bomb that landed in the locomotive sidings near platform 10 was surrounded by four wagons full of ballast to absorb any blast should it explode. When it did explode the morning after, it killed two men.

At Broad Street, the terminus next door, a bomb exploded and threw an LMS goods wagon onto the roof at Liverpool Street, from where it could only be removed by being dismantled. Before the Blitz ended, in May 1940, the offices at Liverpool Street also suffered severe damage.

King's Cross, which had led a charmed life during the First World War, was far less fortunate during the Second World War. It handled some very long trains, with twenty or more carriages being commonplace, so that many of the carriages stood outside the station. Such trains could often have as many as 2,000 passengers, often with corridors crowded with standing passengers.

Early on 11 May 1941, towards the end of the Blitz, two 1,000lb bombs, chained together, dropped onto the west side of the station, exploding and demolishing much of the general offices, the grill room and bar, and completely wrecking the booking office. Much of the roof was blown out, although fortunately, as elsewhere, the glass had been removed. Had this happened at a busy time, the casualties would have been terrible, but it was during the small hours of a Sunday morning. Even so, twelve men were killed. It was in the nature of wartime railwaymen to overcome such difficulties, and temporary booking and refreshment facilities were soon organised and no trains were cancelled.

On the other hand, because of damage on the Metropolitan Line, through services from King's Cross on the Metropolitan Line to Moorgate, in the heart of the City of London, were suspended from 30 December 1940 and not reinstated until almost a year after the end of the war in Europe.

At King's Cross, accident rather than enemy action was to be the major cause of disruption, as we will see later in this chapter.

The other LNER terminus in London was Marylebone, the last terminus to be built in London, to allow the Great Central Railway access to the capital. Today, after many years as an outer suburban station, it has services reaching as far as Birmingham, but in LNER days it handled a reasonable volume of longer-distance traffic with trains travelling as far as Manchester. The station led a charmed life during the Second World War, with no direct hits and the few incendiaries that dropped nearby were easily disposed of. Nevertheless, the station was forced to close by enemy action from 5 October to 26 November 1940, the longest closure of a London terminus, when Carlton Hill Tunnel was penetrated by high-explosive bombs. In clearing the debris the tunnel was left as an open cutting with single-line working until August 1942. The old Great Central goods depot in London was razed to the ground on 16 April 1941. Later in the war, a flying bomb hit the signal-box at Marylebone, killing two men.

Alone among the railway companies, and as early as 28 November 1940, the LNER board instituted a silver medal for members of the company's staff for acts of bravery in the war, with a design by Gilbert Bayes, bearing the LNER crest on one side and on the reverse the words, 'For courage and resource'. During the war years, no fewer than twenty-two members of the company's staff were to receive this award, two of them for outstanding bravery that saved the town of Soham, in Cambridgeshire, on 2 June 1944.

Driver B. Gimbert and Fireman J. Nightall were handling the 11.40 p.m. goods from Whitemoor to Goodmayes yard, which was diverted to the Colne Valley line to run across country to Ely. The train consisted of fifty-one wagons of bombs, including one with forty 500lb bombs next to the locomotive, WD Austerity 2–8–0 77337. Passing the Soham distant signal at around 15–20mph, the driver saw that the first wagon behind the locomotive was on fire. He sounded the whistle to alert the guard, and then stopped the train at the station end of the goods yard. The fireman alighted and uncoupled the first wagon from the rest of the train, and then rejoined the driver as they took the engine forward. The driver intended to get the wagon clear of any buildings and uncouple it before continuing to the next station. As he passed the signal-box at Soham, he called out to ensure that there were no other trains on the line ahead, but almost immediately the wagon exploded, leaving a crater 66ft in diameter and 15ft deep, and damaging 700 houses in Soham as well as demolishing the signal-box and the station master's house. Fireman Nightall was killed and Driver Gimbert seriously injured. In addition to the LNER medal, both men received the George Cross, Nightall posthumously.

Wagon fires were an accepted hazard of goods-train operation for most of railway history, with hot axle boxes being the main cause and, with so much wood in the structure of the goods wagons of the day, a fire could spread very quickly. Given their highly dangerous load, the two men showed outstanding courage, and had they not taken the wagon away from the rest of the train, the explosion would have set the rest of the bombs off and Soham would have been flattened.

While enemy action was not the cause of the Soham incident, the potential of a train carrying bombs to blow up would have delighted any Luftwaffe pilot. Nevertheless, enemy action did have much to account for. In the autumn of 1943, the 8.45 p.m. express from Liverpool Street to Harwich was steaming slowly between Shenfield and Ingatestone because of an air-raid alert. The driver and firemen noticed a bomb explode in the distance, and this was followed shortly afterwards by a bomb exploding in front of the locomotive. Despite steaming at 25mph or so, there was no time to stop and the locomotive plunged into the crater, with the tender riding up over the footplate killing both men. The carriages, which were full, as this was a popular train for servicemen based at Harwich, were scattered, with some of them tumbling down the embankment, but only one passenger and the forward guard were injured. Restoration of services at this point proved difficult, as a high embankment had to be restored, and that only after the locomotive and tender had been retrieved. This was one point on the network where a diversionary route did not exist, so buses had to be used to provide an emergency service between Shenfield and Ingatestone.

The crew of another LNER express fared rather better. Again in 1943, the mixed-traffic 2–6–2 V2 locomotive No. 4771 *Green Arrow* was heading a lengthy east coast express towards Potters Bar, again at the cautionary 25mph judged safe in an air raid as it passed through a tunnel. The driver and fireman saw the tunnel exit ahead silhouetted in the glare of a shower of incendiary bombs, which were normally dropped in large numbers. The driver managed to stop the train with the locomotive just inside the tunnel, before he and the fireman jumped down and began to extinguish the incendiaries on the track, some of which had already set fire to the sleepers. This all happened while the air raid continued, but their prompt action saved both the track from further serious damage and also saved the carriages of the train from catching fire. The crew then walked forward to check that the track was safe, after which the fireman telephoned the next signal-box to explain what had happened. Afterwards, they returned to the locomotive and set off again, steaming very slowly. All in all, this gallant action had taken just half an hour.

York no doubt qualified for attack during the so-called Baedeker raids of 1942 because of the city's historic importance and beauty, but it was also an important railway junction and railway works as well. Early in the morning of 29 April 1942, the full force of an air raid hit York just as the 10 p.m. King's Cross to Edinburgh express arrived. The passengers were advised to leave the train and seek shelter, but many were slow in doing so as they took time to collect their belongings first. A combination of high-explosive and incendiary bombs struck the station and its buildings, with a number of incendiaries falling onto the carriages of the express, setting them alight. While many railwaymen set to tackling the burning carriages, others started to separate the burning carriages from the rest of the train, and managed to save fourteen of the twenty carriages of a typically lengthy wartime express. The remaining carriages, and several other trains in this busy station, were burned out.

During this 'incident', a signalman who had already had his signal-box put out of action by the bombs, went into the station to help salvage whatever rolling stock he could, and with the help of the crew of a locomotive managed to save some twenty carriages and goods vans. Others salvaged ticket racks and furniture from the station buildings as well as money from the tills, taking these items to the safety of the Royal

Station Hotel. Their actions meant that within a few hours of the end of the raid, a temporary ticket office was in operation.

The LNER in York still had a substantial number of horses for its collection and delivery services, but all of these were saved from their stable in Leeman Road by two railwaymen and a policeman after incendiary bombs set the building on fire. Less fortunate, the round-house engine shed was hit by a high-explosive bomb, which destroyed three of the twenty locomotives inside, including the A4 streamlined Pacific *Sir Ralph Wedgwood*. Despite the severity of the raid, by the evening of the same day, most of the running lines through York were operational again, and all lines were available by the evening of the next day.

The first V-2 rocket to strike the LNER was on 16 September 1944 at Palmers Green, where it damaged the track without affecting any trains, and the line itself was restored to service within twenty-four hours. The part of the LNER system most seriously affected by the V-2 raids was Stratford, where track and marshalling yards as well as rolling stock and buildings were badly damaged.

Most of the incidents on the LNER during the war seem to have been cases that could have occurred in peacetime, although the fact that it was wartime did have an impact on the outcome. Typical of these was the accident on 11 February 1941, close to Beighton station, when a heavy steel plate was displaced on its wagon during shunting, protruding well over the side of the wagon and hitting the side of a passing troop train, killing fourteen soldiers and seriously injuring another thirty-five.

Many of the railway termini north of the River Thames have difficult approaches, with several of them in tunnel until close to the terminus. Gas Works Tunnel was always a major problem for steam trains leaving King's Cross. On 4 February 1945, the 6 p.m. to Leeds stalled in the tunnel and then began to slip backwards towards the station. It eventually ran backwards into the front of the 7 p.m. 'Aberdonian', standing at platform 10. Despite the low speed, the moving coaches rose into the air and demolished the signal gantry. It took two weeks before a new gantry could be installed, causing the termination of all suburban services at Finsbury Park.

CHAPTER 13

'OH WHAT A MESS
– THE LMS'

Not simply Britain's largest railway, but the biggest business in the British Empire, the London Midland & Scottish was almost as dependent on goods traffic as its rival on the Anglo-Scottish services, the LNER. Like the LNER, it was preoccupied with its express traffic, and its poverty between the two world wars was only slightly less than the LNER. The LMS was the only railway ever to operate in all four corners of the United Kingdom, something that its publicity made much of with posters declaring '"This is your way Sir" in England, Scotland, Ireland, Wales.' One of its trains in Northern Ireland had the ambitious title of the 'North Atlantic Express', and ran over the Northern Counties Committee lines from Belfast to Portrush. The LMS even reached the south coast of England through its joint operation of the Somerset & Dorset Railway with the Southern Railway. In Wales, it competed with the Great Western by running mail expresses along the coast of North Wales to Holyhead. In Scotland, it reached Wick in the far north.

The LMS had inherited some early suburban electrification from its predecessor companies and, like the Great Western, had shown an early interest in diesel shunters and even experimented with a diesel multiple unit. The electric trains ran on Merseyside and from Euston to Watford, in both cases using the third-rail system. In cooperation with the Southern Railway, it was developing a diesel-electric locomotive for the future. Unlike the LNER, in addition to its fine express locomotives the LMS did have some good freight and mixed-traffic locomotives which it built in large volumes, of which the famous 4–6–0 Stanier 'Black Five' mixed-traffic locomotive was the best known and most numerous, with no fewer than 471 built between 1935 and 1938. The 'Black Five' was to be well-suited to the demands of wartime. However, for heavy freight demands, it was Stanier's 2–8–0 freight locomotive that was to become the austerity standard.

Such locomotives were to be needed in the coming conflict, but were also essential to the pre-war LMS, it having inherited many ancient and often worn-out goods and branch-line locomotives. In fact, despite its poverty between the two wars, the LMS had done well to update its rolling stock. In other ways, too, the LMS had prepared for war. In 1938, a new ramp had been built at Stranraer so that motor vehicles could be driven straight onto the vehicle decks of the steamers, and this was over-designed so that it was wide enough and strong enough to take heavy tanks.

Nevertheless, the LMS suffered from serious internal problems. It had a clash of cultures between the former London & North Western Railway and the Midland Railway, and it seems that there may also have been a similar clash between head office and some at least of the smaller companies such as the Caledonian and the Lancashire & Yorkshire. It could also have been simply too big to manage efficiently, given its huge size and geographical spread, the shortage of money and the uncertain industrial and economic situation. However, it did have a reputation for building fine locomotives, and its long-distance carriages were regarded as being the very best on any of the grouped railways, even better than the 'Centenary Riviera' wide-bodied stock on the Great Western's 'Cornish Riviera' express.

This was a company with 20,000 passenger carriages, 10,000 steam locomotives, 30,000 road vehicles and, before the outbreak of war, more than seventy steamers either in its own fleet or in fleets, such as the Caledonian, in which it was a partner.

Probably the first major British company to import modern management techniques from the United States, the LMS believed in mechanisation and in science. It worked to mechanise the coaling of locomotives, with large coaling hoists lifting up coal wagons and tipping their contents into the tenders of its large express and goods locomotives, dispensing with the use of smaller wagons or hand barrows which were labour intensive. It also led the way with control centres, which had authority over the signalmen and controlled a larger area, although they did not assume the role of the signalman in the modern sense.

ON A WAR FOOTING

As with the other railways, the war started quietly for the LMS, although the restrictions were as substantial for its passengers as for the other companies' passengers, and arguably even more so than for those travelling on the Southern and the Great Western, as so many of the LMS's passengers were travelling very long distances, so the speed limits and additional stops made an impact.

The company played its part in the massive evacuation of children that started on the eve of war and which affected all of the railways, including London Transport. The LMS share of this was to provide 1,450 special trains and, for the three days of the peak movement, the company's Western Division provided 115 special trains daily, while the Midland Division provided forty-five. There were similar but naturally less-intensive movements from Birmingham, Bradford, Edinburgh, Glasgow, Leeds, Liverpool, Manchester and Sheffield. Each train had to be worked back empty to the station from which it had originated for the next day's work. The impact of these other evacuations on the company's operations should not be taken lightly. As mentioned earlier, Merseyside came second only to London in the number of evacuees and trains, followed by Glasgow and Clydebank, and then Manchester. The LMS was the main railway in all of these centres, and the total number of evacuees and trains for these 'provincial' evacuations outnumbered those for London.

FIGHTING THE WEATHER AND THE CENSOR

In common with the other railway companies, the LMS had to introduce severe cuts to its services and restrict the facilities on offer after the evacuation. As elsewhere, this resulted in much adverse comment in the press. Importantly, this was not all ignorant criticism by people in the general press knowing little about railway operation, for much of it came from the railway press.

In one important respect, the criticism was well deserved, for many of the October 1939 schedules were worse than those of October 1918, when the First World War was still raging. For example, on the busy London to Birmingham service, which on LMS metals was 112.9 miles, the best train in 1918 completed the journey in two hours forty minutes. This had been reduced to one hour fifty-five minutes by 1938, but in 1939 it was stretched to two hours forty-one minutes. Average times were much worse, at two hours fifty-three minutes between Euston and Birmingham in 1918, two hours five minutes in 1938, and three hours ten minutes in 1939. Faring a little better was Manchester, 188.5 miles, which had taken four hours thirty-five minutes by the best train in 1918 and three hours fifteen minutes by 1938, but in 1939 took four hours thirty-two minutes, while again the average times to and from Manchester were five hours ten minutes, three hours forty-three minutes, and four hours fifty-two minutes respectively. Glasgow was another instance of a worse schedule than 1918, when the best train had taken nine hours thirty minutes for the 401.4 miles, compared to six hours thirty minutes in 1938, but nine hours thirty-five minutes in 1939. The average was slightly better than in 1918, at ten hours four minutes against ten hours twenty minutes, but this was still worse than the 1938 average of eight hours six minutes. Those travelling between London and Birmingham, however, had only lost a quarter of their daily trains, down from twenty to fifteen, and this was better than the 1918 figure of eleven trains, while Manchester suffered rather more with a cut from twenty-two trains to fourteen between 1938 and 1939, while in 1918 there had been sixteen trains, as well as losing some of its trains from Marylebone. The number of through trains between London and Glasgow was halved, down from twelve to six, the same as in 1918.

Wartime provides its own problems, but without any corresponding let-up in those that a railway might normally expect. The most serious of these was to prove to be the weather, with some exceptionally harsh winters during the war years. The bad weather that hit the railways after Christmas 1939 was the worst since 1916. It was most severe in the north of England and in Scotland. One day, the train due at Euston at 4.17 p.m. from Manchester, Stockport and Rugby arrived seven hours twenty minutes late, while the train from Liverpool due at 6.08 p.m. was three hours twenty minutes late, and the 'Irish Mail' from Holyhead was four and a half hours late. Emergency buffets were placed at the larger stations for passengers stranded in trains that had been disabled by the weather, or whose trains had been cancelled. Food rationing did not start until early 1940, so adequate supplies seem to have been provided easily, although there must have been some serious disruption to the movement of fresh food.

All in, the LMS alone suffered 238 separate cases of lines being blocked by snow, affecting 1,056 route miles. No fewer than seventy-one trains were blocked by snow drifts, and out of these just fifteen locomotives managed to break free to get help. Especially distressing was the plight of the passengers aboard three expresses that had left Glasgow Central on the morning of 28 January 1940, which were blocked near Beattock summit and then almost buried. They were stuck for five days.

Further south, the cutting between Brock and Garstang was blocked for four days because water troughs meant that snow ploughs could not be used. This was another problem for the running of reasonably fast trains over anything more than a relatively short distance – water. With water troughs frozen, extra stops had to be made, and water could even freeze in the water towers. No Anglo-Scottish expresses could run either by the main line or the Settle and Carlisle route between the nights of 27/28 January and 2/3 February.

The Railway Executive Committee was unable to issue the normal apologies or warnings to intending passengers due to wartime censorship, but got its own back some months later when it issued the following poster:

CENSORED

In peace-time railways could explain
  When fog or ice held up your train

But now the country's waging war
  To tell you why's against the law

The censor says you must not know
  When there's been a fall of snow

That's because it would be *news*
  The Germans could not fail to *use*

So think of this, if it's your fate
  To have to meet a train that's late

Railways aren't allowed to say
  What delayed the trains today

This might sound melodramatic, but a massive German aerial attack, difficult to mount though it would have been given that airfields in France and the Low Countries were not then available, would have been an intolerable burden on top of the other difficulties. As it was, much of northern Europe was equally badly affected by the weather and the Luftwaffe seems to have been snowed in at its airfields, but while weather reconnaissance was to assume considerable importance later in the war, at this early stage the belligerents were edging cautiously around each other, even though there was some hard war-making going on in the air and at sea, 'Phoney War' or not.

Doubtless lured by the peace of the 'Phoney War', like the Great Western the LMS was looking forward to a further season's holiday business, and this despite the fact that on 11 March 1940, anticipating the German invasion of Norway, a substantial part of the north of Scotland was declared a protected area by the War Office. The area included everywhere north of Inverness and Inverness-shire and Argyll west of the Great Glen, although not the town of Inverness itself. This meant that travel to the area was restricted to residents and members of the armed forces, while anyone else had to apply for a special pass.

Nevertheless, the LMS continued to approach the coming summer with considerable optimism. In the spring it published its annual guide, *Holidays by LMS*, with no fewer than 684 pages, including 100 with photographs. It could have been a godsend to the Germans if they had intended to invade. The publication appeared at the beginning of May, and on 10 May the German invasion of the Netherlands and Belgium, and then France, started. The special programme of extra trains for holidaymakers, and for the Whitsun holiday in particular, was cancelled, along with the bank holiday itself.

Also shortly to be curtailed was a programme to build 240 2–8–0 Stanier 8F freight locomotives for the Ministry of Supply to augment the ex-Great Central 2–8–0 locomotives taken up from the LNER which had gone to France with the British Expeditionary Force in 1939. The first of these locomotives were ready by late May 1940, but by this time the situation in France was so bad that they were all retained at home until later, when they were sent to Egypt and the Middle East. Nevertheless, these locomotives were to provide the blueprint for the Second World War 'standard' freight locomotive and be built not only by the LMS, but also by the other main-line companies for their own use.

ACCIDENTS

As with the other companies, the wartime blackout imposed considerable difficulties in train operation. The LMS was unfortunate to suffer one of the first serious accidents in which the blackout was a contributing factor. On the night of 13 October 1939, the 7.50 p.m. Euston to Stranraer boat train was running double-headed, but despite having four drivers and firemen on the two locomotives, they managed to pass no fewer than six adverse signals. While the train was due to stop at Bletchley, it approached the station at such speed that it could not stop before it hit a shunting engine that was attaching carriages to another train. In the resulting collision, four people were killed and manslaughter charges brought against the driver of the pilot locomotive, although he was found not guilty.

The fireman of the pilot engine admitted that he had become disorientated and did not realise where he was until the engine exploded detonators at Bletchley, while the experienced driver of the train engine had simply left the duty of watching for signals to the driver of the pilot locomotive. As at Norton Fitzwarren, the situation was confused by parallel tracks. The Chief Inspecting Officer of Railways, Lt-Col Mount, was convinced that the conditions of working in the blackout were substantially to blame for the accident.

It is for consideration whether, and to what extent, blackout conditions on very dark nights affect the normal efficiency of enginemen. It has been stated that such conditions actually make the driver's task easier, and it is true that the 'pattern' of lights today as compared with the maze of different lights which may be observed in peacetime on the approach to a big station or town, is generally confined to a few signals relating only to the line on which the train is running, and perhaps to a parallel line, as at Bletchley.

On the other hand, experience shows . . . the clarifying of the resulting signal 'pattern' has not the safety value it otherwise would have, as the landmarks, by which the driver instinctively locates himself, are also eliminated under blackout conditions. If locating objects, even signal-boxes, are no longer visible, a driver . . . may well lose his whereabouts temporarily, and for sufficient time to permit of speed in excess of that corresponding to signal indications. . . . On moonless or cloudy nights a driver in the blackout speeds through almost impenetrable darkness, relieved only by the lights of signals. The assessment of distances between signals is uncertain . . . drivers may be at considerable disadvantage in assessing their speed and location, particularly after years of operation at 70–80mph, and it is not inconceivable that, without a speedometer, speed may be allowed to rise.

His main conclusion was that the extension of automatic train control was to be pressed ahead with as far as wartime shortages of labour and materials allowed. He also lamented the fact that only on the Great Western were speedometers fitted to locomotives. Amid the conflicting demands and pressures of wartime, his recommendations were ignored.

On 5 March 1940, a more easily understandable accident occurred on the Highland main line between Aviemore and Slochd summit, a difficult section at the best of times. Two 'Black Five' locomotives were double-heading an unfitted mineral train of thirty wagons and a brake van, giving a total of 460 tons, from Aviemore to Slochd, but as it approached Slochd it was stopped at the home signal and then diverted into the down loop line. At this point it was realised that there were only nine wagons, and that the guard's van and twenty-one wagons were rolling back down a 1 in 70 gradient towards Aviemore. The theory was that the guard's van should have been able to hold the wagons if a coupling broke, but this was impossible against such a gradient and, realising this, the guard jumped from his van, suffering injuries as he did so. The signalman at Slochd was slow to realise that there was not a complete train, but then telephoned the box at Carr Bridge 5½ miles away, where the gradient was 1 in 60. The signalman at Carr Bridge saw the train race past his box and could do nothing more than send the 'obstruction danger' signal to Aviemore, where another northbound double-headed goods train had just departed. As this train was 2½ miles north of Aviemore, the crew of the leading locomotive saw red lights approaching, but before they could do anything the runaway wagons crashed into them, overturning the pilot locomotive and killing the crew. Fourteen of the wagons and the brake van were destroyed.

There was another accident on the London Midland & Scottish in late autumn 1940 at Wembley station. At 7.10 p.m. in the darkness of the blackout, a four-wheeled luggage barrow with around half a ton of goods and luggage for a down slow train was being manhandled by three porters up the ramp at the end of the platforms for the up fast and down slow lines. The barrow was overloaded because the porters were trying to move the contents in one move and as a result it was heavier than they could manage. As they went up the ramp, they slipped, and despite their best efforts, it ran back and fouled the up fast line just as the 11.50 a.m. express from Liverpool to London approached, travelling at about 55mph. The locomotive struck the barrow and it is believed that possibly only the bogie wheels of 4–6–0 'Patriot'-class locomotive No. 5529 were derailed initially. The driver acted quickly to close the regulator and apply the brake, but beyond the platform lay a double cross-over leading from the fast to the slow lines. On reaching the cross-over, the locomotive derailed completely, overturned and the weight of the carriages behind jack-knifed the tender, killing the driver and fireman. Fortunately, the train consisted of modern carriages, confining serious damage to the leading three coaches, in which four passengers were injured, but on the platform another nine people were killed.

Only a limited amount of clearance work could be carried out in the blackout and, with wreckage scattered over all four tracks, Euston was closed to steam services, although the electric service to London could continue. It took a week before full services could be restored.

Although this accident has been attributed by some to the blackout, even in normal circumstances the locomotive driver would have had little chance to react. The accident to the barrow occurred just before his loco-motive reached it and, in any case, a bend and a road bridge obscured the view of the station for trains on the up line.

WARTIME OPERATIONS

The LMS share of the evacuation trains for Dunkirk was forty-four, and while this was far from the highest contribution, some of these trains had to convey troops as far north as Aberdeen.

No fewer than 50,000 LMS workers joined the Local Defence Volunteers, and when the title was changed to Home Guard in July 1940, the LMS organised a ceremonial naming of a 'Patriot' class 4–6–0 locomotive No. 5543 at Euston by Lt-Gen Sir Henry Pownall, inspector general of the Home Guard.

To save fuel and wear and tear on track as well as locomotives, the maximum speed permitted was reduced to 60mph, although on the main long-distance routes of the LMS this was later increased to 75mph. The increase in speed was accompanied by drivers being told to use their locomotives to the limits of their ability to make up for lost time. Some drivers interpreted this instruction in the spirit in which it was intended, and even with trains of fifteen carriages or more managed to make up lost time, but others were content to maintain the scheduled timings.

For almost ten months, the widely anticipated bombing did not come, with only a few small-scale raids. While this soon changed with the Battle of Britain as the Luftwaffe tried to put the Royal Air Force out of action prior to an invasion of England, the LMS was sufficiently well away from the main fighter bases in the south of England to have been little troubled at this stage of the war, but all this was set to change with the Blitz, the heavy air raids that started in late 1940 and continued through the winter to early summer 1941. At first, the tactics consisted largely of area bombing, taking a particular town rather than specific targets. Even so much serious damage was done; at Coventry in November 1940 and Liverpool in May 1941 every possible route in the area was damaged, but hard work by repair crews meant that line closures could generally be measured in hours rather than days.

The air raid on Coventry on the night of 14/15 November 1940 saw the LMS suffer no fewer than 122 incidents on its lines around the city. Traffic between Euston and Birmingham had to be diverted at Rugby and sent via Leamington and Kenilworth, returning to the main line at Berkswell. Nevertheless, within two days one platform was again available at Coventry station and the London to Birmingham trains returned to their usual route, using the Coventry avoiding line, a week after the raid. The fact that the Great Western also served Birmingham ensured that there was some flexibility in the arrangements.

From the railway point of view, the worst raid was that of 10/11 May 1941, when a 1,000lb bomb shot through the roof of St Pancras, continued through the floor of the station, itself basically a deck of wrought-iron plates on wrought-iron main and cross-girders, resting on cast-iron columns, and buried itself in the London clay below, exploding when some 25ft down. The explosion created a large crater at the concourse end of platforms 3 and 4 but, even more seriously, it destroyed the tunnel carrying the Metropolitan Line and the Midland trains to the City for about 20ft. Clearing up the mess and starting repairs was made difficult by the presence of an unexploded bomb halfway along platform 2. Nevertheless, undamaged platforms were used and within seven days, with the exception of two platforms, all lines were working again.

The LMS had four London termini: Euston, which was also the company's headquarters, and had been inherited from the London & North Western Railway; St Pancras, built by the Midland Railway; Broad Street, built to give the LNWR access to the City; and Fenchurch Street, originally built for the London, Tilbury & Southend Railway, which was acquired before the grouping by the Midland Railway.

Euston was missed by the Luftwaffe, but even before the heavy raid that so battered St Pancras, Broad Street had suffered badly. On the night of

3/4 October 1940, the lines into the terminus were wrecked by bombing and the station had to be closed for several days. It was hit yet again on 13 October and 11 November. The station had also served the LNER with services reaching it over the lines of the former Great Northern Railway; these had been suspended from mid-September to early December 1939 to make space for essential war traffic, but were ended completely on 4 October as a result of the damage done by the previous night's bombs. Services to East London were cut back after the heavy bombing resulted in many residents being evacuated from what was, in many places, a wasteland. After 14 May 1944, services were not worked east of Dalston Junction.

Fenchurch Street, on the eastern side of the City of London, was relatively unscathed, but services to North Woolwich were abandoned after the bombing of October 1940.

Apart from the occasional closure of London termini due to enemy action, the inner suburban stations at Shoreditch and Haggerston had to be closed for the duration in 1940.

One town that was an obvious target for the Luftwaffe was Barrow-in-Furness, in what is now Cumbria but was then part of Lancashire. Barrow had a major naval shipyard, Vickers, specialising in building aircraft carriers and submarines, although the port itself was owned by the LMS, having been part of the dowry on grouping from the Furness Railway. This was also the site at which many of the pontoons for the Mulberry Harbour were built. During the Blitz of 1941, the hydraulic power system in the docks was badly damaged and sheds along the dockside destroyed. The main casualty was the old Central Station with its all-over roof, and this was completely demolished, the only British railway station to suffer such extensive damage.

To cripple a railway, it is not always necessary to damage buildings, track or trains, as control centres play a vital role, especially when the system is under pressure, when their essential overview can help to maintain services. Each division of the LMS had its own control centre. That in Manchester looked after the Central Division, consisting mainly of the former Lancashire & Yorkshire Railway lines. The emergency room had been built 30ft below ground level with heavy bombing in mind. Just before Christmas 1940, a heavy air raid was under way when a reservoir in the vicinity was breached by a bomb and water began to flood into the control centre. Fortunately, those present were able to escape without serious loss, but operations were hampered as instructions for anything out of the ordinary had to be sent by car or by motorcycle dispatch riders until the control centre was made operational again.

The LMS was the only 'mainland' railway company to operate in Northern Ireland, through the Northern Counties Committee, with its lines from Belfast to Londonderry, Portrush and Larne. Many in Northern Ireland believed that they would be safe from aerial attack because of the distance from the nearest German bases, but in 1938 the senior manager in Northern Ireland, Major M.S. Speir, insisted on building air-raid shelters in Belfast as well as strengthening the signal-box. The Luftwaffe did not mount a major air raid on Belfast until April 1941, which destroyed the company's general stores and parcels office, as well as the audit office and the engineer's drawing office, but the signal-box survived. On 4 May there was a further raid, which cost the Northern Counties Committee twenty carriages and 270 goods wagons, but control and communications remained intact.

On the other side of the Irish Sea, Liverpool was raided for seven consecutive nights in May 1941. During this period, on two occasions the railway network serving the city lost every route in and out of the area, and at one time no fewer than 500 roads were cut.

Such raids obviously resulted in many members of the LMS workforce being killed or injured and seniority was no guarantee of survival. On the night of 16/17 April 1941, Lord Stamp, the company's chairman, was killed in an air raid. This was a loss for the railway companies as a whole since he was involved in negotiations with the government which at the time was cutting back on its earlier deal to compensate the railways. The loss of Lord Stamp, and the fear of being viewed as unpatriotic as invasion threatened, combined to stifle railway opposition to the government's revised proposals.

The general running down of the railways during wartime owed much to the shortage of materials and skilled manpower and, of course, to the extra demands placed upon them, while the available resources were stretched to cover war damage. These factors, vitally important as they were, were only half of the story. Another factor was the use of railway workshops for war production. The massive LMS workshops at Crewe were largely turned over to tank production, building four Covenanter tanks per week, and the reduced wartime output of three new steam locomotives per fortnight soon began to fall behind. At Derby and Wolverton, production lines were set up for the production and repair of wings for Handley Page Hampden and Avro Lancaster bombers. Barassie, the former Glasgow & South Western Railway works in Scotland, had a landing strip built so that it could undertake the repair of damaged aircraft, with at one time 500 women working on damaged Spitfire fighters.

Despite all of this activity, it was to the LMS's credit that in 1941, its works repaired fifty-four 'Black Fives', 119 'Royal Scots', 193 'Jubilees' and 'Baby Scots', and thirty-eight of the massive Garratts. Even so, routine maintenance at the locomotive sheds was less thorough than it had been in peacetime, while wartime loads were much heavier, and the quality of coal provided could never be guaranteed. Such strenuous operating conditions soon began to expose inherent weaknesses and strengths in the different locomotive classes. The cracking of locomotive frames became a problem, and not just with the older locomotives, as this affected a substantial number of the famous 'Black Fives'. One oddity that could never be explained was why, despite having almost identical frame designs, the 5X 4–6–0s gave little trouble, while the 'Baby Scots' proved troublesome. The 'Baby Scots' soon became very unpopular with the footplatemen. Fractured frames meant that a major overhaul took around fourteen days, compared with the six to eight days that under wartime conditions was the standard for more robust locomotives.

Once the United States entered the war, convoys bringing American troops across the Atlantic placed an extra burden on the railways, and the LMS in particular. It was often not known until the last minute whether convoys would head for Liverpool or for the Clyde, with the landing spot often being changed at short notice.

COLLISION COURSE

As the accident at Bletchley showed, the railways were quite capable of adding to their problems without enemy help. Just after the end of the war in Europe, on 21 July 1945, the 1 p.m. express from Glasgow to Euston was travelling at around 60–65mph as it approached Ecclefechan, south of Lockerbie, when it ran past a distant signal at caution and then overran the home signals, to collide with a goods train that was setting back into the down siding (the train ran 'down' to the border and then 'up' to London) to allow the express to pass. The express locomotive, No. 6231 *Duchess of Atholl*, a non-streamlined 4–6–2, finally stopped on its right side, 138 yards on from the point of collision, with the locomotive badly damaged and both its crew killed. The locomotive of the goods train was moved forward 100 yards. Aboard the express, thirty-one passengers were injured.

One result of this accident was that smoke-deflecting plates were added to the 'Duchess' class locomotives, as in wet weather the smoke and steam from these locomotives tended to cling to the boiler top, obscuring the view for the driver. Cautious drivers would frequently cut off steam so that they could see the signals, but those anxious to make up time were less likely to do this.

Shortly after the end of the war, on Sunday 30 September at Bourne End, the up Perth sleeping car express approached a cross-over with a speed limit of 25mph, where it was to cross onto the slow line because of engineering work on the fast line, but took the cross-over at more than 60mph. The locomotive, 4–6–0 'Royal Scot' No. 6157 *The Royal Artilleryman*, managed the sharp turn out off the main line to the left, but then overturned at the following sharp right-hand turn onto the slow line, before plunging down a low embankment dragging much of the rest of the train behind it and onto the top of the locomotive. The death toll was thirty-eight, including the driver and fireman.

THE FERRIES

For all of the railway companies other than London Transport, shipping was part and parcel of their operations. The LMS was no exception, and its main shipping routes were those across the Irish Sea. The LMS also served the shipping services of other companies, including those from Liverpool to Belfast and Dublin.

Its own ships were used on the company's three shipping services to both parts of Ireland. The 'Irish Mail' service from Holyhead used the three 25-knot steamers *Cambria*, *Hibernia* and *Scotia*, while the *Duke of Argyll*, *Duke of Lancaster*, *Duke of Rothesay* and *Duke of York* worked the Heysham–Belfast service. A further three ships, *Princess Margaret*, *Princess Maud* and *Princess Victoria*, worked the short route between Stranraer in Scotland and Larne. On the outbreak of war, the government immediately requisitioned six out of these ten ships, leaving *Cambria* and *Hibernia* at Holyhead, *Duke of Lancaster* at Heysham and *Princess Margaret* at Stranraer.

Princess Victoria was fitted out as a minelayer, and ironically struck a German mine in the North Sea, sinking with heavy loss of life. The other ships were used as troopships, with the first priority being the movement of the British Expeditionary Force to France. This was accompanied without any loss, but a different story arose during the evacuation of the BEF from Dunkirk. The *Scotia* was so heavily bombed while at her moorings that she had to be abandoned before she sank. *Princess Maud* was also badly damaged, but survived, and after Dunkirk was sent to Valery-en-Caux to evacuate further troops with the *Duke of York*; between them they brought back more than 2,000 men safely with little further damage. The *Duke of Argyll* is believed to have taken part in the evacuation of the civilian population from the Channel Islands, before becoming a hospital ship.

Princess Maud was soon returned to the Irish Sea so that she could move men and equipment between Stranraer and Larne, and this traffic proved so intense that she was soon joined by the SR train ferries *Shepperton Ferry* and *Twickenham Ferry* being used as vehicle ferries.

PART OF THE COUNTRY'S MANUFACTURING BASE

All of the railway companies were major manufacturers in their own right, with the London Passenger Transport Board being the exception, buying its rolling stock from manufacturers such as Metro-Cammell. The 'Big Four' were not above buying from outside, but they also maintained a steady flow of work through their own workshops. Even while the LMS was completing its work on the special 'Coronation Scot' London to Glasgow express, the War Office approached the company asking it to design a medium tank. During the Second World War the works at Crewe and Horwich became major centres for tank manufacture.

CHAPTER 14

THROUGH THE HEART OF THE BLITZ

As noted earlier, the inclusion of the railway operations of the London Passenger Transport Board in the government's compensation scheme dismayed the main-line companies, largely because they expected travel on the London Underground to fall during the war years. There was also the wider issue that the compensation scheme was inadequate for the demands being placed on the railways and was inflexible – indeed, the revised scheme was even worse than the original.

While the wartime London Underground system was smaller than that of today, most of the network was already completed, while extensions to the Piccadilly and Central Lines were well advanced. There were two different types of railway comprising the London Underground, with the only two factors in common being the use of standard-gauge track and the London Underground third- and fourth-rail electrification system.

In 1939, the famous deep-level lines, appropriately enough known as the 'Tube' by Londoners and visitors alike, were the Northern, Bakerloo, Piccadilly and Central lines. The Northern and Bakerloo lines had been extended northwards between the wars. The Northern Line was no longer 'the Hampstead Tube' having been taken through Golders Green to Edgware and also having gained two largely surface branches when the LNER suburban branch lines to East Finchley and High Barnet were electrified and taken over for Tube operation. To the south, it was extended to Kennington so that the former 'Hampstead Tube', and the City & South London Line could become one integrated system, and allow trains to run the entire length of the line from Edgware to Morden. While today's Northern Line is very much as it was during the war years, and unique in that it divided to take two routes through central London running via the West End or the City, the Bakerloo was more extensive then than today, having subsequently lost its Stanmore branch in the creation of the Jubilee Line. The Central Line was shorter, with its extension through the East End and into Essex not completed, but the tunnels had been finished and were to be put to good use in wartime. The Piccadilly Line was also shorter, lacking the Heathrow extension, but pre-war had a branch line from Holborn to Aldwych, closed for the war years and now gone for ever, although it was returned to service after the war.

Not included in the Tube system was the Waterloo & City Line, which uniquely was owned and operated as a self-contained line by the Southern Railway and is covered in Chapter 10.

The other lines lay just below the surface, having been built on the less expensive 'cut and cover' system used by most underground railways worldwide. Such lines were to prove extremely vulnerable to bombing, but did not penetrate the central area because even at the time of their construction, London was so heavily built up and the roads already so congested that the widespread use of cut and cover would have been impractical. In any case, being constructed at a time when road vehicle sizes and weights, especially axle weights, were so much lower than today, they would have needed extensive reconstruction for modern needs.

The sub-surface lines consisted mainly of the Metropolitan and District lines with the Hammersmith & City Line, while the Circle Line ran over the tracks of the first two, and the Hammersmith & City ran over the Metropolitan Line to Liverpool Street. The Hammersmith & City Line was, until railway nationalisation in 1948, owned jointly by the Great Western Railway and the London Passenger Transport Board, as successor to the Metropolitan Railway. The East London Line, today shown on underground maps as a separate entity, was at the time part of the Metropolitan Line.

The continued independence of the Waterloo & City Line and the semi-independent status of the Hammersmith & City Line were anomalies. It is indeed curious that neither was completely absorbed by the LPTB on its formation in 1933, since some of the tube extensions entailed taking over surface railway branch lines, and the LPTB had even cut out depots and routes from bus operators on the fringes of its area. It would also have been logical to have included the North London Line in the LPTB network.

While the rolling stock used on the sub-surface lines was built to a different loading gauge compared with that of the Tube lines, the carriages were still shorter than the longest in use on the main lines. The

Metropolitan Line still used steam locomotives for its services as they ran westwards through rural Buckinghamshire, but for a long time had used electric engines for the sub-surface sections, although carriages throughout at the time were non-corridor slam-door compartment stock rather than the sliding-door open cars used on the Hammersmith & City, District and Circle lines. The District and Metropolitan lines still offered first-class accommodation, and the Metropolitan even had two Pullman cars.

When wartime restrictions started to bite, the Metropolitan and District lines lost their first-class compartments on 1 February 1940, but the Metropolitan had already lost its two Pullman cars on 7 October 1939, in order to increase the carrying capacity of the trains. As with the main-line railway companies, services were cut back, although there were often substantial movements of service personnel on the Underground lines, especially between the main-line termini.

LONDON AT WAR

The London Underground faced two conflicting problems during wartime. The population of the London Passenger Transport area actually fell by 2.7 million to 7,147,000 between 1939 and 1944, largely due to evacuation and this, together with the reduced travel caused by the blackout and German bombing, initially reduced traffic substantially. On the other hand, movement of forces personnel brought heavy and sometimes unpredictable traffic peaks, while for service personnel from the British Empire and, later, the United States, even without the bright lights London continued to be the prime destination when on leave. This service-leave traffic was encouraged with the offer of a ticket, costing 1s, which gave visiting service personnel the use of most of London Transport's bus, tram, trolleybus and Underground services for a day, starting at 10.30 a.m.

Because of the original mass evacuation of children, the war started busily enough for the Underground network, with London Transport and the four main-line railway companies told to make arrangements to evacuate 1¼ million people, mainly children, although in the end only 600,000 were moved. While the main-line companies handled the real evacuation, London Transport was responsible for getting them to the departure stations, which were usually not the main-line termini, and in addition to the Underground system, more than 5,000 buses were used.

This was at a time when fuel supplies to London Transport's bus services were cut by a quarter, although to some extent this was offset by the cancellation of the cross-London Greenline-limited stop bus network, with the Greenline 'coaches' converted to ambulances. The number of standing passengers on buses was increased from five to eight, the legal limit at the time, but the cuts in services meant that the Underground, contrary to expectations, became busier. Many commuters started to cycle for part of their daily journey, and at suburban stations London Transport introduced arrangements wherever space allowed for these to be left at the station during the day. At some of the interchange stations in central London, snack trolleys were introduced for service personnel.

In common with the surface railways, the London Underground was badly disrupted by the bad weather that started after Christmas 1939 and continued throughout January 1940. The surface sections suffered and despite de-icing and steel brushes being fitted to trains in passenger service, conductor rails often re-froze between trains. In one case, a train was stalled at Osterley on the Piccadilly Line, having left Hounslow West at 4.13 p.m. The following train was coupled to it a quarter of an hour later, but despite scraping the rails, they froze again before the trains could move very far. Eventually, both trains arrived at Northfields at 11.45 p.m. In normal conditions, this journey would have taken ten minutes.

PROTECTING THE SYSTEM

Preparing for war imposed some engineering and logistical feats on the London Transport railways. The deep-level Tubes may have seemed safe and secure from German bombing, but they had an Achilles heel in that both the Northern and Bakerloo lines ran under the River Thames, with both having their own lines between Charing Cross (now known as Embankment) and Waterloo, and the Northern also running between Monument and London Bridge. At the time of the Munich Crisis in 1938, when a sudden outbreak of war, possibly without prior declaration, was widely expected, the Bakerloo and Northern line tunnels under the Thames were plugged with concrete, but this was a temporary measure.

Early in 1939, plans were drawn up for floodgates on either side of the Thames to protect the lines running under the river, needing eighteen floodgates, each weighing almost 10 tons, and much of this work was completed before the outbreak of war, although the Northern Line between London Bridge and Moorgate did not reopen to traffic until May 1940, having been closed for the previous eight months. The practice was to be that on receipt of an air-raid warning by a traffic office at Leicester Square, the gates would be closed as soon as the line they protected was free of trains, something that could be verified by track circuiting. Closure of the gates took just a minute, and procedures were put in hand to allow the severed sections of line to continue to work independently. In the case of a gate malfunctioning, steel diaphragms were placed nearby, but the gates could be worked manually if necessary.

There were also additional floodgates, smaller and weighing just 4.5 tons each, at Charing Cross to isolate the passages leading from the District and Circle lines to the Northern Line. Further floodgates were installed at vulnerable sections of the District and Circle lines as far west as South Kensington, while on the East London section of the Metropolitan Line, vertical-lift floodgates were installed at the southern end of the Thames tunnel. Elsewhere on the system, precautions were taken to protect it from burst water mains and sewers.

A further line of defence was the positioning of detector devices on the bed of the Thames as a safeguard against acoustic mines that could be set off by the noise and vibration of a train running through a tunnel.

Electricity supply cables were duplicated to ensure continuation of supply in the event of bomb damage.

Disused deep-level Tube stations were used by the government, including the Railway Executive Committee, which took over Down Street station on the Piccadilly Line, it having closed in 1932. The Aldwych branch was closed for the duration of the war and used to store equipment and other valuable items, including much of the collection from the British Museum, among which were the Elgin Marbles. The unopened Central Line tunnels for the extension eastwards into Essex between Leytonstone and Gants Hill were used as a factory for the defence equipment manufacturer Plessey, and a narrow-gauge railway line was laid so that supplies could be moved quickly and easily to the workbenches and completed work taken away. The tunnels provided 300,000sq ft of floor space and were used by 2,000 people working day and night shifts.

The deep-level Tube tunnels soon became a popular spot for those seeking shelter from the air raids once these became heavy during 1940. This practice was discouraged at first, but Londoners started to break into Tube stations after they had closed for the night, and finally the authorities gave in. Officially, the station platforms were allowed to be used from 7 September 1940, and sanitary and drainage arrangements were installed quickly at eighty-one stations, with sewage pumped to the surface. Most of the 'shelterers' slept on the platforms, but in due course bunks were provided for 22,800, although the peak population in the shelters, reached on 27 September 1940, was 177,000, with another 17,000 using the extensions to the system that still had to be brought into use. Admission to the Tube stations was by ticket, provided free by the local authority on a permanent season ticket basis, or on a nightly basis by the ticket office at the Tube station if space permitted. Arrangements were even made for feeding the shelterers, sometimes by the Salvation Army, but there was also a 'Tube Refreshments Special', a converted Tube train carrying supplies to 124 canteens set up throughout the system. All in all, at the peak 120,000 people were fed each night by one means or another.

Many of the inner-city Tube stations became so overcrowded that special trains had to be operated to disperse 'shelterers' to less busy stations. There were also strict rules on how close to the platform edge the 'shelterers' could sleep while trains were still in operation, with them having to pull back 4ft from the edge after 6.15 a.m.

However, the shelters weren't always as safe as the public imagined.

CAUGHT ON THE TUBE

No one expected the sub-surface lines, sometimes referred to by London Transport as the 'surface' lines, of the Circle, District, Metropolitan and Hammersmith & City Lines to be safe from heavy bombing. Indeed, having been built on the 'cut and cover' technique, these lines ran in and out of the open, with some of the stations even having glazed roofs.

An early casualty was Praed Street on the Circle Line, a convenient station for travellers to and from Paddington. On the night of 13 October 1940, just after 11 p.m., three bombs landed in Praed Street itself, outside the Great Western Royal Hotel. The first two exploded in the street, causing considerable damage to the surrounding buildings, but the third exploded on the Circle Line Underground station, which at the time was fairly busy with many passengers waiting for trains. Girders and large wooden beams crashed down into the station, adding to the chaos and the casualties. Immediate rescue came from the air-raid precaution (ARP) personnel of the Great Western Railway at Paddington station, so that all of the casualties were at hospital within an hour or so.

An early indication of what could happen even with the deep-level Underground of the Tube lines came on 12 October 1940 at Trafalgar Square station on the Bakerloo Line, when a bomb penetrated the pavement and killed seven people. The next day, another bomb struck Bounds Green on the Piccadilly Line, causing part of the station tunnel to cave in and killing nineteen people, while another fifty-two were injured.

There was even worse to come. On 14 October 1940, a bomb pierced the station tunnel roof at Balham, fracturing water mains which flooded both tunnels and swept gravel and other debris into the station, killing four London Transport staff and sixty-eight shelterers. The Northern Line had to be closed for three months, compared with the ten days or so that was more usual in other cases of bomb damage. Earlier that evening, London Transport's headquarters at 55 Broadway, under which lay St James's Park station on the Circle and District lines, received a direct hit. On 21 October, the line between Edgware Road and Addison Road was closed owing to severe bomb damage and never reopened.

Given the concerns over the system's vulnerability to flooding, there was a near escape on 12 November 1940, when the station at Sloane Square on the District and Circle lines, which had only reopened after rebuilding some eight months earlier, was destroyed by bombs. A conduit carried the West Bourne stream over the station, and it was fortunate that this was not broken, otherwise a substantial section of this busy line, along which lay no fewer than six main-line termini, could have been flooded.

At Waterloo, the sub-surface booking hall for the Bakerloo and Northern lines was badly damaged on 5 January 1941. However, the worst incident of all came on the night of Saturday 11 January at 7.57 p.m. During a long air raid that lasted from 6.25 p.m. to 9.30 p.m., with 145 enemy bombers operating over London, a high-explosive bomb was dropped by either a Junkers Ju88 or a Heinkel He111, and this crashed through the road into the circular subway under the surface of Bank station, before exploding at the top of the Central Line escalators, destroying the ticket hall and three escalators, and blowing out the windows of two trains standing on the Central Line platforms. Yet again, a water main was fractured, and lighting failed as far as Holborn station, 1½ miles away. Three minutes later, in the blackout, a bus on route 21 crashed into the crater. Inevitably, there were heavy casualties, with four London Transport personnel and fifty-three other people killed, while three London Transport personnel, fourteen passengers and fifty-two others were injured. Many would have been people who believed that they were safer underground than on the surface.

There was little impact on the Waterloo & City Line as the service was suspended due to the problems at Waterloo, but the Central Line service was stopped immediately, and then resumed at 7.11 a.m. the next morning, although for a period trains ran through Bank station without stopping, and then made stops for passengers who reached the platforms by way of the Northern Line station at Monument, with which there were connecting pedestrian tunnels. It seems incredible that it only took two months to restore Bank station to working order.

This time, the Royal Engineers had to take over repair work, creating a box-girder bridge 164ft long to carry road traffic across the large crater between Queen Victoria Street and Poultry to Cornhill and Threadneedle Street. The RE were able to do this using large prefabricated assemblies that had been built and put in stock before the war ready for just such an eventuality.

Yet another major interruption to services came after the exceptionally heavy air raid of 10 May 1941, with damage that resulted in a five-month suspension of services between King's Cross and Euston Square on the Circle and Metropolitan lines.

Nevertheless, the worst loss of life on the British railway system of the war years had little to do with enemy action. At Bethnal Green on 3 March 1943, the still unopened Central Line station was being used as an air-raid shelter, and as the warning sounded, the local population headed for what they thought would be safety. A woman carrying a baby tripped as she went down a short staircase of just nineteen steps, with the press of those behind meaning that others fell. Within a few minutes, 173 people were killed by suffocation and crush injuries.

Despite the difficulties of using deep-level Tube stations, further deep-level station platforms were built below some existing stations on the Northern and Central lines, with no fewer than eight of these at an average depth of 80ft below ground level built at Belsize Park, Camden Town, Goodge Street, Stockwell, Clapham Common, Clapham North and Clapham South, as well as at Chancery Lane. In all, ten were originally proposed, with the hope that with the return of peace these could form part of a deep-level express Tube network – the progenitor of today's much delayed 'Cross Rail' scheme. These new extra deep-level tunnels were built in pairs and were 1,400ft long, far longer than that needed for even a surface train, were of 16ft 6in diameter with a floor built halfway up, and each location had 8,000 bunks fitted. These were ready from 1942 onwards, but first used in mid-1944. Each end of the section of tunnel had a double spiral staircase and a lift for five persons – completely inadequate had an express Tube network ever been built.

The two deep shelters that were not built were to have been at the Oval on the Northern Line, where the water table was too close to the surface for work to proceed, and at St Paul's on the Central Line, where an Act of Parliament prohibited construction of such works so close to the cathedral.

The threat from the air was taken very seriously indeed. Even the deep-level Tubes ran for some considerable distance on the surface, such as between Golders Green and Edgware on the Northern Line which, except for a short length of tunnel north of Hendon Central, ran on the surface. Between Hendon and Golders Green the Northern Line ran much of the way overground on embankment or viaduct.

As on the surface railways, colour light signals had to have extra-long hoods fitted. Also with blackout in mind, on all lines, train windows were covered with cream netting, except for a small area in the centre. The cream netting gradually turned black. Many passengers found it tempting to peel off small areas, and advertisements featuring a character called Billy Brown then appeared in Tube carriages with the message:

> *I trust you'll pardon my correction*
> *That stuff is there for your protection.*

There was further advice to passengers, warning them not to leave a train between stations during air raids or after an alert had been sounded unless requested to do so by a member of staff. One can only assume that such advice was intended for those on the sub-surface lines or while travelling on the surface, as getting out of a deep-level Tube train between stations while in a tunnel would have been impossible. Gas attacks were widely anticipated, and the advice was to close all windows and ventilation, not to smoke, not to touch any exterior part of a car and, of course, always to carry a gas mask.

London was the primary target for both the V-1 and V-2 flying bombs and, not surprisingly, no fewer than 149 of these 'revenge' weapons fell on London Transport facilities. The first of these came in mid-June 1944, when the viaducts carrying the District and Piccadilly line tracks between Hammersmith and Ravenscourt Park were badly damaged. While the engineers managed to restore train services, albeit at low speed, just two days later another V-1 landed close to the point of impact of the first and caused further damage, so that it was six weeks before full services could be restored.

Overall, the war years saw the London Underground system suffer more than 2,000 incidents resulting in damage to the infrastructure, and there were 1,050 cases of damage to rolling stock, with nineteen railway carriages completely destroyed. As with the surface railways, massive arrears of maintenance built up as the workshops went over to war work, including making parts for tanks and armoured fighting vehicles, and the overhaul and modification of more than 500 armoured fighting vehicles. The main effort, however, was in aircraft manufacture, including more than 500 Handley Page Halifax heavy bombers, built by people of whom four-fifths had no previous engineering experience. Perhaps the oddest part of this effort took place in the subway running from Earl's Court station to the exhibition hall, where a part-time voluntary work factory was established in mid-June 1942 to produce aircraft components, and which continued its work for three years, not closing until after the war in Europe had ended.

London and the London Underground survived the Blitz, despite there being only one night without an air raid from 7 September 1940 for the next sixty-five nights, and that was because of bad weather. Yet, bad though it undoubtedly was, it could all have been much worse. Some years before the war, the Luftwaffe had decided to produce large numbers of dive-bombers and medium bombers rather than the heavy bombers favoured by the British and Americans. This was because it believed that success lay in having large numbers of smaller bombers, and because it was easier to produce such aircraft in quantity than the heavy bombers. There was also the point that the German *blitzkrieg* strategy, popularly believed to refer to heavy bombing, actually referred to tanks and aircraft operating in close coordination to create 'lightning war', so that German armies could advance rapidly and overwhelm defences. Thus it happened that a single German bomber could rarely carry much more than a 2,000lb bomb, and it was not until 1943 that the only German heavy bomber, the unreliable Heinkel He177, became available in small numbers.

Contrast this with the RAF's ability to send more than a thousand heavy and medium bombers out over Germany later in the war. The British 'heavies' could carry a 4,000lb 'cookie', and the Lancaster and Halifax could carry an 8,000lb 'double-cookie'. Towards the end of the war, specially modified Lancaster bombers could carry a 12,000lb 'Tallboy' or, still later, a 22,000lb 'Grand Slam' bomb. It was not simply the greater weight and explosive power of these last two bombs that was impressive. They were designed to spin on leaving the aircraft so that they could burrow their way deep into the ground before exploding.

There might not have been a London Underground system had even a handful of such bombs been available to the Luftwaffe in 1940 or 1941. Even the deep-level Tube lines would have been gouged out and doubtless the resulting mess would have been flooded with water and sewage. Had just 4,000lb bombs been used, incidents such as those at Balham and the Bank would have become commonplace. Even these would have been enough to bring the system to a complete halt.

The surface lines of the 'Big Four' would have fared little better. Waterloo would have been especially vulnerable with its approaches mainly on viaduct and the station itself built up high with cellars underneath. St Pancras, built on a deck, would also have suffered disproportionately. These were not the only vulnerable termini, with London Bridge and Liverpool Street being others. The tunnels at Liverpool Street, King's Cross and Euston could all have been blocked, closing the stations for months.

CHAPTER 15

COUNTING THE COST

When referring to the wartime record of the railways in 1944, Sir Alan Mount, the Chief Inspecting Officer of Railways, was able to say that it represented 'an eloquent tribute to their efficiency, standard of maintenance, and on the high factor of safety attained, all of which reflects the greatest credit on every railwayman and woman for the part they played in this historic year'. As we will see in the next chapter, these comments late in the war by an impartial public servant were ignored by the politicians.

It is hard to judge just how much railway passenger traffic was affected by the war since the available statistics do not show the average length of journey, which was likely to have increased considerably. The number of originating passenger journeys on the GWR in 1938 was 129 million, but by 1944 this had increased to 190 million. On the LMS the figures show a smaller rate of increase, from 421 million to 456 million, itself down 2 million on 1943, but static on the LNER at 281 million, again down on 1943. The big exception was on the Southern, where passenger journeys fell from 361 million to 347 million, owing in no small part to the loss of the holiday and excursion traffic. For all of the railway companies, the number of coaching train miles fell between 1938 and 1944, including empty stock workings. These figures tell little of the reality of wartime railway travel, as the number of passengers per train mile increased substantially between 1939 and 1943, without taking any account of the length of journey made, which seems to have increased substantially, still less the amount of time spent aboard the train. On the Great Western, passengers per train mile rose from 3 to 5.6; on the LMS from 4.1 to 6.5, the LNER from 3.8 to 5.4, and on the Southern from 5.6 to 7.6.

Freight ton-miles increased overall by 46 per cent between 1938 and 1943, with the biggest increase, 86 per cent, in merchandise, which doubtless included manufactured items such as munitions. While coal and coke traffic only rose by 13 per cent, the length of haul rose by no less than 30 per cent. In peacetime, there must have been a great deal of one-way traffic, no doubt owing to the private-owner wagons, since loaded goods wagon miles rose by almost a third between 1938 and 1943, and empty miles fell by around 8 per cent. The average load per wagon also rose from 3 tons pre-war to just over 4 tons.

The statistics are inadequate since they consist of totals provided by each company, not by the Railway Executive Committee, so that, for example, a train from, say, Portsmouth to Rosyth could count as four trains, running over the Southern, GWR, LMS and finally the LNER. Nevertheless, passenger specials for the government rose from 24,241 in 1940, doubtless boosted by the Dunkirk evacuation, and after a drop in 1941, to 47,381 in 1943. Freight specials showed a steady increase, from 20,888 in 1940 to 45,583 in 1943.

Naturally enough, throughout the war the hostilities took their toll on railway staff, many of whom continued to work under conditions that many would regard as incredible today. Not only was serious damage repaired as quickly as possible, sometimes with military help, to maintain services, but locomotives and trains were moved to safety during the height of air raids, and many continued to work amid burning buildings. In one celebrated case, a signalman remained at duty in his box despite a naval mine-clearance team working on an unexploded landmine outside!

For the railways' other businesses, including the docks, the picture was mixed, with shipments at many ports falling dramatically between 1938 and 1943, especially for those on the east coast of Scotland and England. They also fell at the South Wales ports. Coal shipments at Southampton increased, but overall traffic was down – Liverpool and Glasgow were safer alternatives for the convoys and the troopships – and of course the cross-Channel and Channel Islands ferry traffic from Southampton, with the latter also from Weymouth, had disappeared.

Overall, in 1935–7, the five railway undertakings had average annual total operating receipts of £195,236,000 and expenditure of £158,500,000, which gave them net operating receipts of £36,727,000 and net revenue of £39,903,000. By 1944, the annual figures had risen to total operating receipts of £394,360,000 and expenditure of £301,200,000, giving net operating receipts of £93,193,000 and net revenue of £90,256,000, but, of course, of the last figure, they were only allowed to keep £43,469,000, with the rest going to the government. Overall, for 1941–4 the railways received a total of £173,876,000 and the government received £176,199,000, and these figures ignore the sums for 1939–40 and for 1945.

THE STATE OF THE RAILWAYS

In 1943, at the annual general meeting of the Great Western Railway, shareholders were told that the arrears in repairs and maintenance had reached £8.5 million, about a third more than the Great Western's guaranteed annual compensation for the use of its track and trains. The growth in arrears did not represent negligence on the part of the company, but instead it was a reflection of the shortage of materials and skilled manpower.

Some relief for the hard-pressed railway came in 1943, with the arrival of 2–8–0 tender freight locomotives from the United States, to be pooled by the 'British Railways', a title that was being used repeatedly. Assistance in the reverse direction came when ambulance trains converted from its own rolling stock by the Great Western were handed over to the United States Army. The American freight locomotives did not stay long before they were taken back and sent to support the United States Army after the invasion of Europe.

When it came, the end of the war was a relief, long expected after the invasion of France and seemingly often delayed. Unfortunately, the travelling public expected the service to return to normal as soon as possible, despite the damage and the arrears of maintenance and renewals which by this time on the Great Western alone had reached no less than £18 million, equal to some £540 million at today's prices. This sum was almost three times the annual compensation still being paid to the company. The annual compensation arrangement was intended to continue for at least a year after the cessation of hostilities. Nowhere was the continuing impact of the war more obvious than with the ferries, for as 1945 dawned, there was just one Great Western ship not in government service.

Perhaps the easiest way to describe the impact of the war years on the travelling public post-war was that not only did the trains look neglected and war-stained, and even battered, but that reliability had also suffered badly. The Great Western maintained that pre-war it had suffered a locomotive failure once every 126,000 miles, but in the immediate aftermath of the war it experienced a failure every 40,000 miles.

Unfortunately, the Great Western's management was soon to discover that the company would not receive even the normal peacetime allocation of materials, let alone that regarded as essential to make good the war damage and catch up on maintenance and renewals. A good example was that in 1938 the permanent way teams had used around 19,000 cast-iron rail chairs, yet in 1946 the Great Western was allocated just 12,500 rail chairs by the Ministry of Supply. This was despite the GWR estimating that 25,000 rail chairs a year would be needed for three years to bring the track back to the pre-war standard. The rolling stock situation was also grim. In 1938, the Great Western had a total stock of 6,168 carriages, and of these 5,819 were available for service every day, but by 1946 the total stock had dropped to 5,738 carriages, and of these just 4,441 were available for service owing to the backlog of repairs. This meant that the company had gone from 94.3 per cent passenger rolling stock availability to just 77.4 per cent of a much lower total. The carriages that were left were also much older, as the average age had risen from eighteen years to twenty-two years.

The Great Western's experience was typical of every railway operator, even the nationalised London Transport, although only a relatively small proportion of the country's population used its services regularly, if at all. On the Southern Railway, the winter period had seen many trains heavily overcrowded, and punctuality fell far short of the pre-war standard, forcing it to resort to a poster campaign and press advertisements to explain its position. A good example of the impact of wartime was that in January 1946, the 2¼ route miles between Waterloo and Queen's Road, identified by the railway as its most bombed stretch of track, had no fewer than four severe speed restrictions, three to 15mph and one to just 10mph. Needless to say, the state of the track was also reflected in the poor state of the rolling stock, with frequent breakdowns, while on the Eastern Section at Victoria, the number and lack of regularity of military leave specials had an impact on the normal services. In December 1945, the electric trains, at one time noted for their punctuality, had an average delay of five minutes.

The chairman raised these matters at the 1946 annual general meeting, held in March. He told the shareholders that the restoration of normal services could not be done quickly, because of the shortage of materials and of men, with only a quarter of Southern personnel serving with the armed forces having been released by that time. The railway was still running 570 special trains for the government every week, and long-distance traffic was up 480 per cent compared with 1939, yet the quantity of electric rolling stock available was down by 3.5 per cent. While a considerable mileage of track had been renewed in 1945, in 1946 it was also hoped to renew damaged bridges and stations. On a more hopeful note, the chairman also talked of further electrification and explained that the 1935 loans from the government for electrification could now be repaid, even though repayment was not due until 1952.

Nevertheless, the Southern seemed better able than some to cope with its problems. Its management, many of them soldiering on beyond their usual retirement age while they waited for colleagues to be released from military service, turned its attention to improving the railway as it was, and by July 1946 electric trains were suffering an average delay of just one minute.

The railways post-war nevertheless were in the position of trying to do more with considerably reduced resources than they had employed pre-war. If 1938 had been a poor year for the railways, 1946 and 1947 brought an embarrassment of traffic. On the LMS, the average train was carrying 140 per cent of its pre-war loading, with passenger miles up 70 per cent while train miles were down by 30 per cent. Engines, carriages, stations, track, signals and bridges were all worn out, crying out for attention, while the workshops that had given them regular overhauls had been committed to building tanks, guns, invasion barges and aircraft. All of this was aggravated by poor-quality coal, and frequent cuts in the volume of coal affected even such a vital industry as the railways, on whose performance other industries depended.

Probably what counted more was the experience of those on some of the London, Midland & Scottish Railway's branch lines, where intending passengers had to open compartment doors and look inside to see whether there was room for them as the windows were so filthy. An acute shortage of labour had meant that even such basics as cleaning carriages and locomotives were neglected, and in any case many carriages needed what is sometimes described as a 'deep clean'. Many recall the LMS locomotives in particular being so dirty that often engine numbers had to be chalked on to aid identification. Not for nothing did one wit scribble the graffito: 'LMS – a hell of a mess'. Schoolboys delighted in swinging their satchels through the air and against seats to send a cloud of soot and dust into the air of an already murky compartment.

THE WEATHER TAKES A HAND

It almost seemed as if the fates were ganging up on the railways in the two years after the end of the war. One of the worst winters on record came in early 1947. It was inevitable that services were affected both by the bad weather and by the looming shortage of coal. Bad weather kept miners away from work, and the coal that was brought to the surface was often frozen at the pit head and difficult to load. For those rail-ways operating steam locomotives, water was also a problem, as the water troughs were rendered useless by the low temperatures, forcing longer-distance trains to make additional calls to take on water, itself a hazardous task requiring locomotive firemen to climb on top of tenders in freezing conditions and in strong winds. In early February, the govern-ment introduced curbs on the use of electricity by industry, and this extended to the railways, so that starting on 5 February, cuts were enforced on many suburban services, followed on 11 February by a further round of cuts, with still more on 15 February. The massive freeze continued until 8 March when a thaw started, augmented by heavy rain on 10 March that resulted in flooding of many low-lying stretches of line.

The bad weather had started in January. Heavy snowfalls were accompanied by strong gales and, in between, the periods of calm were marked by freezing fog. The Southern's third-rail electrified lines were especially prone to disruption in such conditions and the company responded by introducing de-icing trains, with elderly trailer carriages modified to spread a thin film of warm oil on the third rail sent on a tour of the electrified lines. This worked up to a point in keeping lines open, provided that the intervals between trains was not too long.

However, in the severe gale of 4 March, heavy rain washed the de-icing oil from the third rail, then turned to a blizzard, and the resulting precipitation froze, causing massive disruption. The 4.25 p.m. non-stop from Brighton to Victoria, instead of taking just an hour to reach the capital, took more than eight hours. Throughout the country, many train drivers stopped their trains at stations while waiting for the weather to improve.

If these severe conditions were not bad enough, the massive freeze continued until 8 March, when the thaw started. The Portsmouth Direct, notoriously prone to earth slips, was hit between Petersfield and Rowlands Castle, and the section was reduced to single line working. The line to Sidcup flooded at Mottingham. The Brighton line was also badly affected, as heavy rain caused chalk falls on the approaches to both the Quarry and Merstham tunnels early on 13 March, blocking the former line and leaving the other with just one line clear. The hard-pressed control staff had to introduce widespread cancellations and diversions, including the substitution of a steam train via Oxted for the busy 5.45 p.m. from London Bridge to Eastbourne. It took until 17 March to clear the mess, by which time the heavy rain had caused the fallen chalk to become sticky, damaging the track and the ballast, and its removal had to be followed by extensive reballasting. Elsewhere, the line between Windsor and Staines was flooded, and the line between Eynesford and Shoreham (Kent) was also closed by chalk falls. It took until the end of March before trains could operate normally, and even then the service was still massively reduced by the fuel shortages.

CHAPTER 16

AN UNGRATEFUL
NATION

Do they think that the public will have a better and a cheaper
service? Do they think that the wage earning and the salaried staffs of
the Main Line Railway Companies will be better off? . . . I challenge
the nationalisers to prove their case. I accept the challenge to prove
that public interest can best be served by private ownership of the
Southern Railway.

Col Gore-Browne, 1946

This was fighting talk. Col Gore-Browne was angry and indignant. He was
speaking at the 1946 annual general meeting of the Southern Railway, of
which he was chairman. After putting up such a robust defence of the
railways under private enterprise, in hindsight it seems ironic that just a
year later he found himself defending his actions in the face of criticism
from the shareholders, whose turn it was to be angry. Gore-Browne told
his audience:

Now may I turn to the record of last year and to the plans which we
have in view. Some . . . have asked 'Why as things are now, have you
made any plans? Is not your only duty to protect your stockholders'
interests?' We feel it necessary to take a wider view. We have always
regarded your undertaking as a service to the public . . . the
Chancellor of the Exchequer who described the railways as 'a very
poor bag of physical assets' will in our case be agreeably surprised.

Facing nationalisation from a Labour government with a massive
majority, the Southern Railway's directors and senior management had
continued to plan as if nothing was going to change. Possibly, seeing that
the country had other priorities after a long and financially debilitating
war, the Southern's directors and senior management were hoping for a
last-minute change of heart. Either way, their enthusiasm for renewed
planning and investment had angered many shareholders, and it is hard

not to have sympathy with them, for they had stuck with the company through the lean years of the 1920s and 1930s, when it had developed the world's largest electric suburban network, and electrified the main lines to the Sussex coast and to Portsmouth, as well as vastly extending the docks at Southampton and becoming involved in domestic air transport, only to see the state profit from the Herculean efforts made by the railways in wartime. Every penny spent on modernisation could have been paid in dividends, instead of being invested in new trains, track and signals, when it became instead a gift to the future owner of the railways.

'This railway system of ours is a very poor bag of assets,' Hugh Dalton, Chancellor of the Exchequer, had told the House of Commons during the second reading of the Transport Bill on 17 December 1946. 'The permanent way is badly worn. The rolling stock is in a state of great dilapidation. The railways are a disgrace to the country. The railway stations and their equipment are a disgrace to the country.'

If Britain's railways were such a poor bag of assets in 1946, one might wonder why it was that the lines on the Isle of Wight continued to operate Victorian locomotives and rolling stock right up to 1966, which were then replaced by elderly rolling stock dating from the 1930s that had been withdrawn from the London Underground. The Southern Railway's plans to pick up where it had left off in 1939 and extend electrification as far as possible, with diesel traction for the less economic lines and for what were then known as stopping goods trains, serving small stations that at the time still had their own sidings, were to come to nothing. The Treasury would see to that.

At the time, MPs were discussing the terms of compensation to be paid to the shareholders, and the Chancellor had been pressed to justify the appalling compensation that was proposed. He managed to avoid mentioning the strains of war, but by the time the measure became law, the *Financial Times* was moved to point out that the claim that the railways were a 'poor bag of assets' had been disproved. Indeed, among those with an open mind, the railways were truly war-battered and exhausted. Not only had the system been worked to the limits, and endured heavy enemy aerial attack, but it had also seen its locomotives and rolling stock taken as far away as Persia. At home, hastily trained labour had taken the place of the skilled men who had either volunteered to join the armed forces or had been conscripted. In addition to the shortage of materials and manpower, the workshops had in many cases been given over to war production and, faced with the need to repair bomb damage, the priority was repairing and rebuilding while routine track and rolling stock maintenance had to be neglected.

GREY DAYS

These were grey days for the country as a whole. Much has been made of the return of the bright lights with the end of the restrictions enforcing the blackout by VE Day, but the population had to continue with rationing of almost everything, except one or two items such as fresh fish and bread, which had not been rationed during the war years, *was* rationed post-war.

People had to use public transport. Even if they could get hold of a car, it would be an old one, since with the exception of a few models for military use, car production had stopped for the duration and petrol was difficult to obtain. Buses, including those of London Transport which had come to pride itself on the condition of its fleet and its overhaul arrangements, now included many with holes in their bodywork; others had chassis that sagged alarmingly in the middle. In just under six years of total war, the country had been so battered and its circumstances so reduced that it resembled what would today be described as a third-world state, with little that worked. Large areas of many towns and cities had been razed to the ground, or had the remains of gutted buildings standing bleakly against the sky.

Just how much of the public enthusiasm for nationalisation resulted from onerous wartime travel restrictions and the controls that left the timetable often halved or worse, when additional traffic had to be handled, or journey times extended by a third or more, is hard to say in retrospect. On the other hand, the vote for Labour may not have been a vote for nationalisation but a vote against what many had come to see as the unfairness and inequality of some aspects of British life.

The service restrictions early in the war led the then mayor of Brighton to publicly accuse the Southern Railway of always having treated his town badly. This was despite the fact that it had not only been the first beneficiary of the Southern's mainline electrification plans, but had also enjoyed a more than doubled frequency of trains in the process. He withdrew his accusations when the Southern's directors produced a vigorous response. This was a clear example of how the railways were blamed for government policy.

There were other factors at work. The full evil of the Soviet system had still to be revealed and, post-war, Communism was even respectable. Few people were shareholders and few understood, or even cared, how the system worked.

Apart from enthusiasts, the railways never enjoyed great popularity. The errors and shortcomings of the worst obscured the achievements of the best. This still happens today. In 2003, a reader of *Modern Railways* wrote a letter, tongue in cheek, claiming that he had been cheated of his quota of cancellations, delays and overcrowding on his daily journeys across Yorkshire. At a time when the author commuted daily on the Portsmouth line, there was certainly a spell when the original electrification stock, well past its working life and often showing signs of neglect, created many problems and delays, but once replaced, on-time arrivals occurred on 90 per cent of journeys, and 'on time' in this case meant bang on time, not within five minutes, as with today's punctuality figures. Despite this, people still grumbled and few were appreciative. Part of the problem is, of course, that public expectations of the railways are often unobtainable and unrealistic. One Ministry of Transport civil servant once told the author that the by then nationalised railways were making vast profits out of suburban commuters because the trains were so overcrowded, and refused to believe that if the train then spent the whole day idle in a siding, it was losing money. Most of its peak-hour passengers were enjoying heavily discounted fares anyway, with savings on annual season tickets amounting to 40 per cent on suburban journeys and up to 60 per cent on longer services.

The real problem over the nationalisation debate was simply that the public – the electorate and taxpayers – didn't care.

Who did care then? The railway shareholders were outnumbered by the railway workers. Nationalisation in the UK was driven by the workers in particular industries. Labour was committed to the nationalisation of almost everything, although in later years some prominent ministers would deny that they would nationalise 'down to the last corner shop'. Railwaymen, coal miners, steel workers, all wanted to control their own industries, a series of 'soviets'. Labour also decided that air transport should be run by the state. How shipping managed to remain off-limits is a mystery, although even this was in the sights of later Labour administrations. The docks belonging to the railways were nationalised, but the remainder were left untouched simply because so many of them were in local authority control, or run by public bodies, later leading one

Conservative rebel, Enoch Powell, to propose that the ports should be nationalised so that the situation could then be sorted out and all of them denationalised.

There can be no doubt that the attitude of workers post-war was very much that the railway would soon be 'theirs'. This is not an unreasonable assessment of their attitudes since the establishment of the Railway Executive disappointed many trade unionists because it was dominated by railway managers.

Public attitudes may have been strongly influenced by the wartime restrictions on railway operation, failing to appreciate fully that these were imposed on the railways by the Railway Executive Committee, which in turn was instructed by the Ministry of War Transport and, before it, the Ministry of Transport. In wartime, the railways were for the first time victims of diktat by the Treasury, and it would not be the last time, while the three separate service ministries all had frequent demands on the railways, as did the Ministry of Supply. In fact, the paying public, the regular traveller, the voter, the customer, all really just one category, came bottom of the heap. But it was not the fault of the railways.

The neglect of suburban and branch-line travellers on the mighty London Midland & Scottish and the not quite so mighty, and poverty-stricken, London & North Eastern must have affected the image of the railways. It was not enough to have the fine expresses streaking across the countryside, outside the experience of the vast majority of travellers. It was the day-in, day-out slog on a slow and dirty, if not downright dilapidated, branchline train or an overcrowded suburban train that stuck in the memory. There is a general accord that the LNER achieved much with its suburban services, and with steam locomotives that could, in the case of one class, match the performance of electric trains for acceleration, and perhaps even outperform them when the rails were wet or slippery, but electrification had been promised and electric trains were cleaner, but, most of all, *they were modern*, the buzzword between the wars. Times were changing. They not only had electric trams, but also electric buses with the silent efficiency of the trolleybus, while the first electric household implements were finding their way into the more affluent homes. For many, the radio had arrived, and for the few, the television made an appearance shortly before the outbreak of war. Not only that – the passenger enjoying first class travel on the Coronation Scot or the Flying Scotsman could well have a connection with one of the grimy branch or suburban trains, or might have travelled on the gleaming new electric trains of the Hampstead Tube, now renamed the Northern Line, or on 1938 Circle Line stock, all part of *the* London Transport. Perceptions are all.

Even the Great Western, treating both classes of passengers decently and with its diesel railcars on the branches, still depended on steam for its admittedly small London commuter business.

The undereducated and unthinking masses had the vote and intended to use it. The affluent liberal-minded were attracted by the efficiency between the wars of the nationalised European railways. It mattered not at all to them that Mussolini had made the trains run on time in Italy by demanding realistic timetables, and not by improvements in efficiency. In Germany, where things were efficient and becoming more so, Britain's railways were shown up when the Great Western's 'Cheltenham Flyer', at one time the fastest regular train in the world, lost its crown to the German Berlin and Hamburg express. Meanwhile, in the United States, steam was fast losing its crown to diesel, and it didn't occur to the educated elite that in that country of vast distances and infrequent long-distance trains, the railways were already losing the battle for not just long-but intermediate-distance travellers to the airlines. The Douglas DC-3 or C-47 transport plane, known in the UK as the Dakota, had originally emerged as the DST, or 'Douglas Sleeper Transport', to carry passengers overnight across the United States.

Nationalisation of the railways overnight gave the state control of the main ports, plus the railway hotels, haulage firms such as Carter Peterson and Pickfords and the travel agency Thomas Cook. It provided a substantial ferry and coastal shipping fleet and a large number of bus companies, especially when the state also managed to absorb the bus interests of Thomas Tilling, Scottish Motor Traction and the British Automobile Traction Group. The government's priority was nationalis-ation, greater state control and a cradle-to-the-grave welfare state, rather than reconstruction and improvement of the manufacturing base and infrastructure. These assets were all acquired cheaply, but they had been neglected out of dire necessity during the war and, in the immediate post-war period, the railway companies could not even obtain their usual peacetime allocation of materials for routine maintenance and renewals, let alone make significant inroads into the massive backlog.

The new British Railways started life on 1 January 1948, with 19,639 route miles of track, a small fall in route mileage since 1930 partly due to some minor pre-war trimming of the network and wartime closures of unnecessary routes. BR inherited 20,023 steam locomotives, 36,033 passenger carriages, plus a further 4,184 carriages contained within electric multiple units, and 1,223,634 goods wagons, of which half had been privately owned prior to nationalisation and with which, as already mentioned, the outgoing railway companies had been compelled to share their compensation, even though many belonged to the soon to be nationalised coal mines and steel works! There were small numbers of diesel railcars and shunting engines.

At first, the boundaries of the old Southern Railway and the Great Western approximated to those of the new Southern Region and Western Region. There was some tidying up, with Fenchurch Street transferred to the new Eastern Region, while joint lines were each allocated to the most appropriate region. The LNER was divided between the Eastern, North Eastern and Scottish regions, and the LMS between the London Midland and Scottish regions. In effect, the east coast and west coast main lines in many ways reverted to what was almost a pre-grouping structure. On the Southern Region, the old pre-grouping structure continued in the three divisions, Eastern, Central and Western, that perpetuated the areas of the South Eastern & Chatham, London Brighton & South Coast and London & South Western railways.

Sir Eustace Missenden, the last general manager of the Southern Railway, chaired the British Railways executive. It was to be an unhappy end to his career on the railways – the job had been turned down by his counterpart on the former Great Western, and Missenden was soon to understand why. Instead of making decisions and answering to shareholders, he found that his hands were tied and investment could be vetoed by the Treasury. Beneath the chairman, the executive comprised functional officers who issued directions to their counterparts in the regions, each of which had a chief regional officer to act as a representative of the executive on the one hand, and a coordinator of the departmental or functional officers on the other.

The newly nationalised railways had an operating surplus of £19 million (£356 million today) in 1948, small enough given the size and turnover of the undertaking, but by 1955 this had become a deficit of £17 million (around £238 million today). The deterioration was blamed on rising costs and renewed road competition, as well as an industrial dispute that seriously affected the railways throughout a substantial part of 1955, and doubtless gave a shot in the arm both to the road competition and to the expanding internal air services.

The railways were war-battered, as indeed were so many of Britain's towns and cities, but they were far from being a 'poor bag of assets' post-war. Much of the rolling stock and locomotives inherited by the new British Railways survived for many years, with one of the most extreme examples being on the Isle of Wight where, until the end of steam in the 1960s, the system consisted of Victorian locomotives and rolling stock. Steam locomotive production continued so that when steam was finally withdrawn in 1967, some locomotives were scrapped at less than eight years old. From the early 1950s onwards, line and station closures became increasingly common, even before the infamous Beeching cuts of the 1960s and 1970s. It would be very difficult for the railways of today to face a crisis such as the Second World War with the same robustness and flexibility.

CHRONOLOGY

1939

January

29   ARP exercise in early hours at London Paddington.

May

26   Military Training Act requires all railwaymen between ages of 20 and 21 years to register.

August

Annual general meeting of the National Union of Railwaymen at Abergavenny in Wales in mid-August decides to formulate pay claim, with threat of strike action.

24   Minister of Labour meets railway unions to persuade them to call off strike planned for 26 August.

31   Evacuation of children from London and other centres ordered.

September

1   Government seizes control of the railways, anticipating the outbreak of war, with the Emergency (Railway Control) Order.

1–4   Evacuation of children and nursing and expectant mothers from London and other cities. Railways carry 600,000 from London.

2   Blackout ordered by government.

3   Outbreak of the Second World War in Europe.

11   Maximum speed restriction of 45mph introduced.

11   Massive reductions in railway passenger services lead to protests. Catering facilities and Pullman cars withdrawn on the main lines.

16   Through working of trains between the Great Western and the Metropolitan Line ended.

18   Cuts in timetables reversed on week days.

25   Revised timetables issued for both the Great Western and London Midland & Scottish.

October

Maximum speed raised to 60mph.

2   Revised timetable for the London & North Eastern.

7   Pullman cars withdrawn from the Metropolitan Line.

13   Serious accident at Bletchley involving double-headed boat express and shunter, with four fatalities.

16   Revised timetable for the Southern Railway.

December

Canadian troops begin arriving and are moved by rail to their barracks.

2   Further revised timetable for the London & North Eastern, including additional restaurant cars.

1940

Construction of 100 350hp diesel shunting locomotives authorised on the LMS. January sees severe weather with many trains cancelled and others stranded in snow drifts. The winter months see floodgates installed to isolate the sections of the Northern and Bakerloo lines and the East London Line that run under the River Thames.

January

1   Pullman cars and restaurant cars reinstated on Southern Railway.

28   Three expresses running south from Glasgow stuck in snow drifts at Beattock for five days. Settle & Carlisle route closed by snow.

February

1   First-class travel ends on Metropolitan and District lines.

2/3   Settle and Carlisle line reopened.

7   Minister announces financial agreement with the railways on compensation for state control.

March

5   Accident north of Aviemore when heavily loaded wagons from a goods train break away and run into a following train, killing the crew of the pilot locomotive.

11   Most of northern Scotland declared a prohibited area and closed to visitors.

May
During this month, fares were raised by 10 per cent to help cover the mounting costs of the railways and to discourage travel.

18 Weston, Clevedon & Portishead Light Railway closed after being bought by the Great Western at the Railway Executive Committee's bidding.
19 Second evacuation of children from coastal areas of Southern England begins.
23 *Maid of Kent* and *Brighton*, marked as a hospital ships, sunk after being bombed.
26 'Operation Dynamo', the evacuation of the British Expeditionary Force from Dunkirk, ordered.
27 Start of the evacuation of the BEF from Dunkirk.
29 *Brittany* requisitioned, but by noon government demands all steamers of more than 1,000 tons with a range of 150 miles.
30 *Scotia, Lorina* and *Normannia*, operating as military transports, all sunk at Dunkirk.

June
During this month, Captain Euan Wallace is replaced as Minister of Transport by Lord Reith. System of compensating the railways for wartime role is changed and war damage no longer reimbursed. After the fall of France, the Romney, Hythe & Dymchurch Railway is handed over to the Royal Engineers.

2 Hospital ship *Paris* bombed. 48,000 children moved from east-coast towns using seventy trains.
4 Dunkirk evacuation ends. Isle of Wight paddle steamer *Whippingham* carries 2,700 men from Dunkirk.
12–18 Further evacuation of 100,000 children from London to Wales and the West Country.
17–28 Evacuation of the Channel Islands takes place.
19 Channel Islands declared a demilitarised zone. Southern Railway engineers' works at Redbridge destroyed by bombs.

July
1 Southern Railway workshops at Dover requisitioned by Admiralty.
10 Train bombed near Newhaven, Sussex.

August

16   Bombs block two lines near New Malden, Surrey, killing railway-men and passengers.

September

7   Londoners allowed to use deep-level tube stations as air-raid shelters.

7–19   Waterloo station closed as a result of bombs damaging the approaches.

27   Peak occupation of Tube stations, with 177,000 people using these as air-raid shelters.

October

3/4   Broad Street station closed for several days by bombing.

5   Marylebone station closed until 26 November after Carlton Hill Tunnel penetrated by a bomb, blocking access.

12   Trafalgar Square station on the Bakerloo Line penetrated by a bomb, killing seven people. Southern Railway power station at Durnsford Road badly damaged by bombing.

13   Bounds Green station on the Piccadilly Line penetrated by a bomb, causing part of the station tunnel to cave in, with nineteen deaths and fifty-two injured. Broad Street station again closed by bombing.

14   Balham station on the Northern Line penetrated by a bomb which also fractures water mains, killing seventy-two people.

21   Line between Edgware Road and Addison Road closed due to severe bomb damage.

November

4   REC closes the Van Railway on the Great Western.

11   Broad Street station again closed by bombing.

12   Sloane Square station on the District and Circle lines badly damaged by bombing.

14/15 Heavy raid on Coventry with no fewer than 122 'incidents' on London Midland & Scottish lines in and around the city. Trains have to be diverted for a week after the raid.

28   London & North Eastern Railway directors agree to institute LNER Medal for bravery shown by the company's employees during wartime. Eventually twenty-two awards are made.

December
During this month, Lt-Col J.T.C. Moore-Brabazon becomes Minister of Transport.

8   Bomb causes extensive damage and flooding to the Waterloo & City Line, which is closed until 15 April 1941.

12   Landmine lands at London Bridge near signal cabin, but does not explode and work continues while it is defused.

29/30 London Bridge station badly damaged by incendiary bombs. Waterloo closed for a time by fire bombs. Through services from the LNER at King's Cross to Moorgate suspended because of damage to the Metropolitan Line and not reinstated until after the war.

1941

January
5   Bomb wrecks booking hall for Bakerloo and Northern lines at Waterloo Station.

11   Bomb penetrates road at Bank Underground station and explodes at the top of the Central Line escalators, killing fifty-seven people and injuring sixty-nine. Power lost as far as High Holborn.

11/12 Portsmouth Harbour station bombed, wrecking train and viaduct so that station is cut off from the network for the rest of the war.

February
11   Maximum speed increased to 75mph. Near Beighton station, steel plate on goods wagon strikes troop train killing fourteen and injuring thirty-five.

April
7   Chancellor of the Exchequer assumes control of railway fares and freight charges.

16/17 Lord and Lady Stamp and eldest son killed by German bomb. Landmine falls on Hungerford Bridge, and Charing Cross badly damaged by bombs. Bridge over Southwark Street destroyed by bombs, and lines into Blackfriars and Holborn Viaduct cut. Bomb damage to sub-station at Waterloo closes Waterloo & City

Line until alternative power arrangements can be made. Metropolitan and Circle Line so badly damaged between Euston Square and King's Cross that it is out of action for five months. Ex-Great Central London goods depot razed to the ground by incendiaries.

19   Underground lines running under the Thames closed for a short period while the river is swept for mines.

May

Ministry of Transport becomes Ministry of War Transport and assumes control of shipping from the Board of Trade, while Lord Leathers of Purfleet becomes the new minister.

4   Heavy air raid on Belfast costs the Northern Counties Committee of the LMS twenty carriages and 270 goods wagons.

10/11 Worst night of bombing. Waterloo and Cannon Street damaged, Holborn Viaduct gutted and out of action until 1 June, Elephant & Castle badly damaged, Waterloo & City Line flooded and out of action until 22 May. King's Cross badly damaged by two 1,000lb bombs. St Pancras badly damaged in bombing, with several platforms out of action for a week.

June
13   Great Western packet *St Patrick* bombed and sunk with heavy loss of life while on passage from Rosslare to Fishguard.

September
20   Paddle steamer *Portsdown* mined and sunk while on passage between Portsmouth Harbour and Ryde.

October
6   All suburban services within the London Transport area become third class only.

1942

May
US troops begin to arrive and are moved by rail to their barracks and training grounds.

22   All catering facilities withdrawn except for some West Country trains on the Southern Railway.

25   Bomb destroys one of the piers of a viaduct at Brighton, cutting the line to Lewes.

October
Train heating reduced.

5   All cheap day returns withdrawn.

9   New bridge over Southwark Street completed.

December
Sleeping cars no longer available for civilian passengers.

1943

March

3   At Bethnal Green, on an unopened stretch of the Central Line, a woman carrying a baby trips and 173 people are killed by suffocation and crush injuries.

1944

January

24   *St David* sunk off Anzio.

April

2   Visitors banned from south coast.

June

2   In the early hours, a train carrying bombs has a wagon catch fire as it passes through Soham in Cambridgeshire. The driver and fireman isolate the wagon before it blows up, killing the fireman.

17   V-1 wrecks a goods train between Elephant & Castle and Loughborough Junction.

Mid- Viaducts carrying the District and Piccadilly Line tracks between
June Hammersmith and Ravenscourt Park badly damaged by a V-1, and

while services are still disrupted another V-1 lands nearby, so that it takes six weeks before services are fully restored.

18   V-1 damages Hungerford Bridge and restricts working at Charing Cross.

July

12   V-1 damages bridge carrying Catford Loop over the South London Line.

29   Crowds force Paddington station to close for three hours.

September

13   Shell lands on Dover Priory station, killing several people.

October

16   Double derailment interrupts normal working at Paddington.

November

2   V-2 puts signalling at Hampton Court Junction out of action for two days.

5   V-2 destroys bridge at Bermondsey.

1945

January

31   Admiralty returns Dover workshops to Southern Railway.

February

4   Train stalls in tunnel at King's Cross and runs back into Aberdeen express standing at platform.

March

During this month V-2 hits a block of Southern Railway flats at Deptford, killing fifty-one people.

May

8   VE Day, a public holiday at two days' notice. Railway freight traffic cancelled.

July

21   Glasgow to Euston express hits goods train at Ecclefechan. Express driver and fireman killed and thirty-five passengers injured.

August

15   VJ Day, with a two-day public holiday only announced at 11 p.m., so the following day many commuters turn up at work.

October

1   Restaurant cars start to be reinstated. Travelling Post Offices reinstated.

1947

February

5   Cuts enforced on suburban services to save fuel.

11   Further cuts to save fuel.

15   Still more cuts.

BIBLIOGRAPHY

Bishop, D. and Davies, W.J.K., *Railways and War since 1917*, Blandford, London, 1974

Bonavia, M.R., *A History of the LNER, Vol. 3, The Last Years, 1939–1948*, George Allen & Unwin, London, 1983

Crump, N., *By Rail to Victory: The story of the LNER in wartime*, London & North Eastern Railway, London, 1947

Darwin, B., *War on the Line: The story of the Southern Railway in wartime*, Southern Railway, London, 1946

Glover, J., *London's Underground*, Ian Allan, London, 1999

John, E, *Timetable for Victory: A brief and popular account of the railways and railway-owned dockyards of Great Britain and Northern Ireland, during the six years' war, 1939–1945*, The British Railways, London, 1946

Nash, G.G., *The LMS at War*, London Midland & Scottish Railway, London, 1946

Nock, O.S., *A History of the LMS, Vol. 3, The War Years and Nationalisation, 1939–1948*, George Allen & Unwin, London, 1983

INDEX